REAL SOLUTIONS
for Overcoming Internet Addictions

REAL SOLUTIONS
for Overcoming Internet Addictions

Stephen O. Watters

VINE
BOOKS

SERVANT PUBLICATIONS
ANN ARBOR, MICHIGAN

Vine Books is an imprint of Servant Publications especially designed to serve evangelical Christians.

All Scripture quotations, unless indicated, are taken from the HOLY BIBLE, NEW INTERNATIONAL VERSION. Copyright 1973, 1978, 1984 by International Bible Society. Used by permission of Zondervan Publishing House. All rights reserved.

The stories in this book are true. In most cases, names have been changed to protect the privacy of the individuals portrayed. In some cases, actual names have been used by permission.

Published by Servant Publications
P.O. Box 8617
Ann Arbor, Michigan 48107

Cover design by David Uttley Design

01 02 03 04 10 9 8 7 6 5 4 3 2 1

Printed in the United States of America
ISBN 1-56955-268-1

Dedication

To Griffin George Watters

We'll have to wait to hold you in heaven.

Contents

Acknowledgements

I'm grateful:

To the men and women who were willing to share
their Internet struggles with me.

To Dr. Jennifer Schneider, Dr. Kimberly Young,
Dr. David Greenfield and the other Internet addiction
pioneers for their research and comments.

To Servant Publications, especially my editors Bert Ghezzi
and Kathy Deering, for pursuing this book topic and
giving me the chance to tackle it.

To Rob Jackson, Steve Earll, Dr. Steve Fetrow, and Dr. Harry
Schaumburg, as well as Willy Wooten and the counseling
department at Focus on the Family for your insight into a
Christian understanding of addiction.

To my parents and brothers for encouraging
creativity in our home.

To my wife, Candice, and our son, Harrison, for giving me a
thousand reasons to get off the computer for the night.

Acknowledgments

Introduction

Internet Addiction: A Real Problem

Brad finally looked up from the screen; the clock read 5:00 A.M. He had done it again. Five hours of Internet porn. No sleep. "Why can't I stop?" he thought.

Mike lit up the dark hotel room with the glow from his laptop. The rest of his family tried to get some sleep after an exhausting day at Disney World. He was on vacation, but Mike just couldn't go a day without checking in on his chat room friends.

Beth rushed to the computer to get on-line. What would her new friend have to say today? Unfortunately, she found her daughter on the computer. In a panic, she dragged her away and eagerly checked for messages.

Mark didn't believe his friends when they said he had a little problem. It was all just fun and games. It wasn't like he was surfing for porn or gambling; he was just playing an Internet game with some friends ... just about all the time.

If This Sounds Familiar ...

Can you identify with these true stories? Have you embraced the excitement and novelty of some area on the Internet only to find yourself on a roller coaster where the highs are followed by the lows of anxious thoughts, guilt, and a growing sense of dependency?

Or are you the person on the outside looking in, watching someone you love abandon you, hobbies and activities, and everything else that used to be important, to spend countless hours staring at a computer monitor?

Maybe you're the confidant a friend turns to with his or her problem: a counselor, a pastor, or an accountability partner. Do you find yourself feeling concerned, but not sure how to help?

If you can identify with any of these situations, this book may be the resource you need to understand a growing problem and begin taking important steps toward recovery, or to help a friend do so. Addiction, compulsion, sinful idolatry—whatever you call it, at its core it's a trade-off. It's a desire for pleasure, control, or escape, despite other requests for your attention—and despite the effects on those around you or to your health, wealth, or reputation.

The temptation is to minimize the problem. Popular culture rarely criticizes Internet overuse or abuse, and even the experts disagree about the Internet's destructive capabilities.

Addiction Debate

Alcohol and drug addiction appear alongside other compulsive behaviors in the DSM-IV (Diagnostic and Statistical Manual of Mental Disorders), the essential handbook of psychological disorders. Yet there is no entry in the DSM-IV for "Internet addiction." Does that mean it's not addictive?

Research hasn't demonstrated a causal relationship for Internet abuse, says Dr. John Grohol on his "Mental Health Net" Web site. Excessive Internet use doesn't make someone an "Internet addict," he insists, any more than being a bookworm makes someone a "book addict."[1] "Breathing Is Also

Addictive," mocked a *Newsweek* headline[2] in the wake of shocking stories about Internet addiction. Forget the hype, many experts say. You can't be addicted to the Internet.

Several mental health professionals disagree. Drs. Kimberly Young and David Greenfield, along with a growing number of colleagues, insist that it should be taken seriously. Young and Greenfield are pioneers in the understanding and treatment of people like Brad, Mike, Beth, and Mark.

"No professional practicing today could say that there isn't a problem with compulsive Internet behavior," says Greenfield, who believes that at least eleven million Americans struggle with it.[3] Young explains that even though there is not a clear chemical dependency, as there is for alcohol or drugs, Internet users can become "psychologically dependent on the feelings and experiences they get" while using the computer.[4] As many as 5 to 10 percent of people on-line experience dependency, according to her studies—a number similar to that for gambling and alcohol abuse.[5] Those viewing pornography or pursuing on-line relationships make up almost half of that number.

So when does frequent Internet use cross the line to become an addiction? "Addiction is when you can't stop, you can't get away from it, and you need to do it more and more often," says Dr. Maressa Hecht Orzack, a Harvard University psychologist who launched McLean Hospital's Computer Addiction Services. "It's craving it when it's not there. It's being depressed, irritable, or angry when you are not on the computer. It's flunking out of school. It's not feeding the children. It's oversleeping after staying up all night on-line. It's neglecting work."[6]

Orzack, Greenfield, Young, and others are gaining ground in their arguments as more and more clients show up to see counselors with symptoms of Internet addiction. It still may be awhile, however, before we see clear clinical definitions for Internet addiction. Dr. Greenfield points out that it took twenty years to get gambling addiction added to the DSM. In the meantime, as you already may have noticed, a lot of people are using the Internet in a way that looks a lot like addiction—creating some real problems that need some real solutions.

Help for the Christian Community

Up until now, unfortunately, the church hasn't been sure how to address Internet problems. When Dane Aaker, an American Baptist pastor in Colton, California, preached his "How to Break Destructive Habits in Our Lives" sermon series last year, he was overwhelmed by the number of people who came to him with stories of on-line addictions—involving everything from endless hours spent surfing and hanging out in chat rooms to full-blown affairs.

Of all these Internet problems, pornography and other forms of Internet sex are without a doubt the greatest threat to families. Shane Womack, another pastor in California, says, "Watching my church and speaking with other Christian leaders, it is obvious that on-line sexual addictions are becoming a massive problem for churches."[7]

Some Christians may be amazed that Pastor Womack uses the word *addiction*. It's not a word you can find in the Bible—how does it fit in with a Christian view of sin versus holiness? Dr. Mark Laaser, a Christian sex addictions counselor, offers a good answer to this question. He says that the word *addiction* helps us to define the qualities of sin: Sin is the lack of a relationship with God and the destructive behaviors that are committed as a result. Sin is unmanageable and causes people to not trust God, to try to control their own lives, and to commit behaviors destructive to themselves and to others. Sin causes us to be ashamed. Sin causes us to die. Unmanageability, escape, shame, and *addiction* are interwoven into the very fabric of sin.[8]

So what do you do about it? Is praying enough? Former addicts say that prayer was only part of their recovery—it had to be coupled with some soul-searching and some specific steps toward healing and discipleship.

Can you fix an Internet addiction by just removing the source? "Just cut the thing off." That's what Bob's pastor told him when he mentioned his Internet porn problem. Yet, while total computer abstinence may be the solution for some, the Internet is too ubiquitous to make this the standard prescription. Would Bob's pastor tell a man struggling with phone sex to simply cut off his telephone service? There's got to be a better, more practical solution.

For Brad, Mike, Beth, Mark, and the thousands like them, this book tries to provide some real solutions. The first half of the book describes for the Christian community the addictive nature of the Internet, specifically in the form of auctions, stock trading services, gambling, interactive games, pornography, and chat rooms.

The second half of the book prescribes some solutions, both for the person whose Internet use is out of control and for the person who knows someone with this problem. Yet, the solutions aren't just about getting a habit under control through behavior modification (a popular secular treatment). True transformation requires a comprehensive focus. A real solution for overcoming Internet addictions requires restoration of not only the body but also the mind, the heart, and the soul.

Chapter One

Trade-Offs: What Addiction Can Do

I've often heard the question, "How do you know when your Internet use has become an addiction and needs to be addressed?" Instead of waiting until an activity becomes an addiction before addressing it, however, a simpler approach is to ask, "How is your 'Internet life' affecting the rest of your life?"

"Think about what makes up your life," says Steve Earll, a certified addictions counselor. "There are your relationships with friends and family, your relationship with God, your hobbies and activities, your work, your health, your reputation, and so forth. The degree that Internet use negatively affects those other areas of your life is the degree to which it is a problem."[1]

Christians are reminded that anything that is not done in faith is a sin (see Rom 14:23). If you know in your heart that your use of the Internet comes between you and God, then your Internet use needs to change—regardless of whether it has reached the level of addiction.

Take a minute right now to reflect specifically on five key areas of your life: your time, your work, your thought life, your reputation, and your relationships. If you honestly assess these areas and see any losses or potential losses that you can attribute to Internet use, you know that you have a problem worth addressing.

Time

America Online recently mailed me a trial-membership offer. I usually throw offers like these away, but this one caught my eye. It offered me seven hundred free hours of Internet time. Seeing this, I couldn't help but think, "Wouldn't it be nice if an Internet provider could offer more than just unbilled Internet hours—if they could actually add free hours to your life?" Yet they can't.

Anyone who uses those seven hundred hours is going to have to take that time away from something else. "[In that time,] you could have planted a tomato garden, volunteered at a hospital, spoken with your child's teacher, and taught the kid down the block how to shag fly balls," says Clifford Stoll, an Internet pioneer turned skeptic.[2] Every hour that you spend on-line replaces an hour you could have spent with friends, with family, on hobbies, and so on. Even activities that are totally innocent can be time wasters.

The Internet now takes up one-fifth of leisure time, according to Cyber Dialogue.[3] Like television viewing, however, there's not always a lot to show for it. The Internet rarely offers the same physical payoff that, say, gardening or building model airplanes can. It sure doesn't burn calories the way walking, biking, or other exercise does. Even worse, it doesn't encourage face-to-face interaction in the way that playing board games or cards would.

Granted, we seldom take full advantage of the free time in our lives. Still, the Internet has a way of consuming larger and larger chunks of leisure time—making it harder to balance Internet time with other, more rewarding, leisure activities.

Mike suspected his Internet surfing and chatting in Christian chat rooms might have grown a little out of control, but he really felt convicted when a pastor reminded him that he would have to give God an account for his money and his time. "I'm not wasting a lot of money, but I am wasting a lot of time," he thought. "I used to read a lot, and was disdainful of people who watched excessive amounts of television, but the Internet is not a whole lot better—I just find myself vegetating there."

One way to put your time into perspective is to do the "sitting in your rocking chair, looking back on life" test. Which moments are you going to recall with greater fondness: Exploring the great outdoors or exploring an imaginary MUD (multi-user domain)? Chatting with neighbors over the fence or chatting with strangers halfway across the country? Taking family pictures or surfing for pictures of fantasy women?

How would you give an account of the time you spend on-line?

Work

People typically have to dedicate around forty hours a week to some kind of work in order to pay the bills. Of all the facets of our lives, work is the one area that financially supports most of the others. For that reason, work is valuable time that you can't afford to compromise. Unfortunately, thousands of people do just that every day.

More and more employers are beginning to feel robbed by their employees' Internet habits. "Cyberloafing" now accounts for 30 to 40 percent of lost worker productivity, according to International Data Corp. "With the world's greatest diversion at their fingertips, many multitaskers are turning into multi-slackers," says Michelle Conlin in *Business Week*, "doing everything from ordering spring wardrobes [to] planning elaborate summer holidays, carrying on torrid cyberaffairs, day-trading their portfolios, and eBaying their belongings."[4] Companies everywhere are starting to crack down on unnecessary Internet use. Twenty-eight percent of companies in a survey by the American Management Association indicated that they had dismissed employees for misuse or personal use of telecom equipment. One of the most notable examples was Xerox, who fired forty employees for inappropriate Internet use.[5]

Employers are especially intolerant of porn surfing, because of their concerns about creating a hostile workplace. In a high-profile move last year, the *New York Times* fired twenty-three employees for sending obscene email.[6] Amazingly, as many as 70 percent of employees admit to either viewing or sending adult-oriented personal email at work.[7] Furthermore, a service called SexTracker has determined that the majority of traffic to many adult sites takes place during work hours. This particular service estimates that "one in five white-collar male workers is accessing pornography at work."[8]

Dr. Jennifer Schneider, an expert on sex addiction, recently surveyed a group of men and women who were being treated for cybersex addiction. One man, thirty-six, married, and a professional, seemed to have no sense of the risks he took at work. "I would spend on the average three hours a day at work behind my closed door cybering and masturbating," he says. "My work productivity was cut by probably 75 percent. I would sit there at work masturbating as secretaries were knocking at my door."[9]

"Sometimes the biggest challenge was to see if I could go on-line and not get caught," said a lawyer who went to Dr. Harry Schaumburg for counseling. "It was almost a game," he added, as he described the multiple violations and warnings he received. Finally, his employer sent him a letter that plainly said, "The next time we find you looking for porn, you're fired." The warning was not enough—he went back and got fired.[10]

Employees who don't go on-line at work can still find their work suffering. They may stay up late at home on-line and have no energy left for work the next day, or they may find themselves constantly distracted by obsessive thoughts about being on-line again.

It's one thing to cheat an employer out of time and resources. It's another thing when you are the boss. Mike found it increasingly difficult to balance his Internet habit with his freelance work. "At the workplace, you have water cooler breaks where you can stop working and chat with coworkers," he says. "As a freelance writer working out of my home I missed that. I'd find myself saying, 'Well, it's 10:30, I think I'll take a break from writing.' I'd minimize my work window, fire up the Internet, and plan to chat with people for about ten minutes. Soon it was like two hours and it was eating into my ability to do my job."

Does your Internet use help or hurt your work?

Thought Life

"I thought about [a multi-user domain] game all the time in college, and it became more important than my grades or my friends," says Mark.

"What scared me the most about being drawn into [on-line porn] again was the constant guilt, all day and all night—it is very scary and debilitating," shares J.B.

"A lot of my friends are failing out of school because of [on-line gambling], because it's all you think about," says Andy.[11]

Your thought life—an abstract place between your heart and head—is often the first area to feel the effects of compulsive Internet use. As Internet use moves toward addictive behavior, three things often begin to dominate your thought life: anxiety, fantasy, and damage control.

The rush and excitement that often come with Internet activities seem inevitably tied to a high level of anxiety. The anticipation and the hunt for a satisfying on-line experience can seriously erode the peace that comes from finding your happiness in God. Perhaps your thought life is now consumed not with hopes and plans for family and friends but with anxious plans to be back on-line—making another trade, viewing another exciting image, completing another level in a game.

Then there's the fantasy. Brad found it increasingly difficult to leave the fantasy world. "I would look at a woman, be able to undress her in my mind, and then could complete my fantasy. These women were completely unaware of what I was doing. It could happen anywhere—at the mall, at work, even at church." It was a guilty yet satisfying feeling for him. If nothing else, it seemed to help him escape from the problems of real life and the complications of real relationships. When life brings challenges, the fantasy world promises a quick escape, an easy fix with a nice numbing effect.

Brad's other mental preoccupation was running damage control. "I was the model Christian guy on the outside—it looked like I had it all together. I was the star player on my high school baseball team. I was president of the youth group at my church. From the outside, anyone else would say, 'this kid's got it all together, he has no problems.' I worked hard to cover my tracks and smooth things over so that I could keep up that image. The fact that I knew better—that I knew what I did last night—really fed the guilt and the shame. That kept me from getting close in relationships, because I thought, 'what if they find out that I'm not the person they think?' I wasn't willing to be vulnerable to that possibility."

Chris was terrified that someone would find out about his secret porn habit. "At night, I had to make sure everything was hidden away before I went to sleep. If I didn't, I would dream that someone came in during the night and discovered my terrible secret."[12]

How is your thought life? Are there gaps between the public "you" and the private "you"? Are you constantly fantasizing? Do you find yourself incessantly thinking about on-line activities during the time that you're not on-line? How much of your thought life is devoted to covering your tracks or worrying about getting caught?

Health, Finances, and Reputation

"The pain at times has been crushing," Jody Burgin told the crowded room of congressmen and reporters. "My [pornography] addictions cost me: my marriage; the role I cherished as Daddy; job opportunities in the field of my calling and choice; legal problems resulting in over $100,000 of fees, retirement income, and support obligations; loss of friendships; [and] loss of credibility and trust. The consequences of pornography affected me emotionally with a deep and permeating sense of shame and guilt."[13]

How could Jody have gotten to such a place? Couldn't he have seen it coming? The siren song of addictive pleasures—combined with the virtual nature of the Internet—often blinds people like Jody to the risks of their actions. The lure of control, wealth, an emotional high, or sexual pleasure compels Internet users to want more. An on-line experience that met a need one session needs to come in a higher dosage the next session to have the same effect.

Reaching a greater level often requires taking risks. On-line gamers may take the risk of skipping college classes or work in order to reach a new level. Gamblers and day-traders may be motivated to risk losses they know they can't cover. Porn surfers may chase fantasies that would shock their spouses.

It all comes down to crossing a line. As soon as the compulsive Internet user thinks the payoff for his or her actions is worth the risks, that person forgets to think rationally about the value of his or her health, finances, or reputation.

Despite all the freebies on-line, there are still plenty of ways to lose money—on auction sites, premium porn services, and gambling sites, for example. One guy found out in the worst way how easy it is to lose money day-trading. Following just one stock, he constantly bought and sold again, watching intently for any movement. In no time, he blew a million dollars that had been left to him by his family, and now he owes the brokerage $80,000.

The Internet doesn't always cause the same kind of health reactions that overeating or abusing alcohol and drugs can. Yet there can be consequences. Carpal tunnel syndrome, dry eyes, migraine headaches, backaches, eating irregularities, failure to attend to personal hygiene, sleep disturbances, and change in sleep patterns all show up on Dr. Maressa Orzack's list of physical symptoms of computer addiction.[14] In survey after survey conducted by Internet addiction researchers, participants have reported fatigue from late-night surfing and stress from compulsive desires to get back on-line. A recent study by the Center for Disease Control demonstrated that a significant number of people who have sexually transmitted diseases use the Internet to arrange sexual meetings.[15]

Julie didn't think about the consequences until after she had sex with a guy she met on-line. "After awhile, I felt bad, like 'oh geez, now I wonder if I have AIDS or some disease.' If they would come and meet with me and have sex, don't you think they do this a lot? It's like no one thinks about this stuff when they get together—it was like a game."[16]

The best way to screw up a good reputation is to get your name in the paper after being arrested. That's what happened to a sixty-year-old man who corresponded with Dr. Schneider. "I got arrested for sending porn to a minor, who was in fact a police officer. I lost my job, articles were in all the papers, and I was on TV. I lost friends. My family distrusts me, some don't even want to see me. I'm facing a jail sentence."[17]

Have your health, finances, or reputation already been damaged? If not, what would happen if your private world and public world collided?

Relationships

As I mentioned earlier, Brad took off to a fantasy world to avoid the complications of real-life relationships. Unfortunately, that happens all the time. We all crave meaningful connections with other people, yet we often find ourselves unwilling to be vulnerable enough with someone else to experience real intimacy. The Internet offers something like intimacy, without so much vulnerability.

"Emotionally I was in a daze for that whole year of being on-line," the twenty-nine-year-old man told Dr. Jennifer Schneider in a survey. "I was occasionally there to support my wife, but I seemed always to be thinking about the next time I could get on-line. Sometimes she'd ask me to pick her up for lunch and I would get angry, making something up about how I had errands to do, so I could stay home and surf. Our relationship became significantly strained. We'd go months without having sex. My wife said she felt extremely alone during that period."[18]

The strain on relationships is one of the greatest tragedies of compulsive Internet use. "We are relational beings at our core—we were created to relate intimately with other people," says Dr. Steve Fetrow, a counselor who focuses on the role of relational breakdown in addictions.[19]

Even the most innocent uses of the Internet can cut into the time necessary to maintain meaningful relationships. The more time people spend on-line, the less time they spend with friends and family. That's what researchers found in separate studies conducted by Stanford and Carnegie Mellon Universities.[20]

Faceless friends in chat rooms, multi-user games, or other on-line communities often become more important to Internet users than the people they know in their life away from the computer.

Mike noticed that the Internet caused him to give up his habit of writing letters to friends. "I found that if my friends weren't on-line, I'd just ignore them. I would write three or four emails a day to new cyber acquaintances, but my old friends who weren't on-line became second-rate friends, and that's a shame. I kick myself about that."

He also found himself putting his marriage and family on autopilot. Every night, he would eat dinner and then head straight for the computer, where he'd stay until midnight or later. "We went on vacation to Disney World," he says, "and I remember thinking 'I can't be away from the Internet for a week.' So I put the Internet software on my laptop system and took it with me. In the evening I would go in the chat rooms and talk to people. I remember one night the lights were off, everyone was trying to sleep, and there I was chatting, lighting the room with the glow of my laptop."

Relationships grow more vulnerable when someone has

something to hide. A marriage built on trust, honesty, and two-way communication can begin to unravel in the face of deception, denial, and blame. A husband may be careful to hide evidence of an on-line gambling habit from his wife, but the secrecy inevitably erodes trust and openness in the marriage.

Relationships are more directly affected by emotional or sexual affairs and obsessive porn use—frequently causing loss of sexual interest in the partner, sexual acting out, and even exposure of children to pornography.

One of the biggest relational problems in Internet addiction is the level of competition the spouse faces when compared to a fantasy person on-line. Whether it's a new friend in a multi-user game, an acquaintance in an on-line community, or even an endless series of airbrushed images and virtual sex encounters, the person on-line comes across as more exciting, less disappointing, and more engaging than real people in the computer user's life. Of course that kind of competition is going to make a spouse seem less attractive.

Dr. Schneider interviewed nearly a hundred people whose spouses had cybersex addictions. She noticed that the respondents consistently reported feeling "hurt, betrayal, rejection, abandonment, devastation, loneliness, shame, isolation, humiliation, jealousy, and anger." She adds that "being lied to repeatedly was a major cause of distress."

One lady in the survey, the young wife of a pastor with an on-line porn habit, wrote, "How can I compete with hundreds of anonymous others who are now in our bed, in his head? Our bed is crowded with countless faceless strangers, where once we were intimate."[21]

Relationship damage is by no means limited to those compulsive users who are married. Dr. Steve Fetrow, a counselor and former youth pastor, explains that singles often use their singleness as an excuse for compulsive behavior. "They say, 'because I'm not in a relationship, I'm not tied to the same rules and guidelines as married people.' However, we were created to relate intimately with other people regardless of whether we are married or not. If singles don't already have meaningful relationships with family, friends, or coworkers, they ought to."[22]

Finally, whether we realize it or not, God is jealous when we let things come between him and us. Throughout the Old Testament, God seeks out a relationship with the Israelites—using metaphors of a bride, a lover, and eventually even a prostitute to describe his jealous efforts to restore a close relationship (see Jer 2:2, 3:2; Hos 3). His heart hurts when we try to fill a God-sized hole with small on-line pleasures. Most importantly, he misses us when we, like Adam, skip the walks and talks in the cool of the day (see Gn 3:8) and instead hide away in our shame.

How are your relationships with friends, family, and God?

Chapter Two

The General Lure

"Just another few minutes." That's what Mike kept thinking as he explored the Internet for the first time. He had signed on after dinner and had planned to spend an hour or so seeing what the growing hype was about. It was the early 1990s and Mike had heard through his computer gaming job about a network of terminals that put gobs of information at your fingertips. Mike was an information guy. "I used to sit down and just read the encyclopedia for fun. At that time, there were very few pictures or graphics on-line, no Yahoo!, no audio, but I was amazed by what I could find." With little effort and no cost, he visited the Smithsonian, the Vatican, the Sistine Chapel, and whatever else he could think of to add to his virtual travel itinerary.

You know the rest of the story. Another few minutes turned into another few hours, and Mike stayed up all night that very first time on-line. The attraction was just too strong. Over the next couple of years, the lure of Internet surfing and later chat rooms grew strong enough that Mike described it as an addiction. "I found myself thinking about it a lot. I was constantly looking for new sites and applications," he says.

He wasn't cruising porn sites. He didn't have an affair. He wasn't gambling or blowing his savings account on day-trading. Did he really have a problem? He tells me that even though he wasn't tied up in any problem areas, at one point he literally couldn't pull himself away from the Internet. I can identify with him. While attempting to write this book I began to develop what I would call at least a compulsive surfing habit.

I wrote this book during the 2000 election season, and unfortunately I'm a political junkie. Last year's pre- and post-election coverage reached a new threshold. To cover the closest race in four decades and the longest presidential contest in over a century, every news outlet had an on-line election feature, and dozens of new services launched their own election sites. For someone eager to find new information on all the close races and then the unfolding drama in Florida, the wealth of sheer political stuff out there was a great temptation. As I began to explore, I found news stories and commentaries, analyses and predictions. I found background information on the candidates—their voting records and their campaign contributions. I found polls and then more polls. Each Web site I reviewed seemed to link to another resource, and another after that. I found reams more information than I ever would have found in the morning paper or on the nightly news.

On top of all the election coverage last fall, I also found out that my favorite musical group planned to release a new CD ... and they had a new Web site. At their site, they had a "studio cam" where you could watch the final recording and editing work taking place. Every other day or so they would add a new feature—new pictures and interviews as well as news and gossip about the work in progress. After a while, they added teaser audio clips and promised to trickle more and more out. I was blown away—I had been buying this group's music for years and I had never been able to hear audio snippets before the album was released. I started checking additional fan sites and found even more stuff—video clips, lyrics, previous concert set lists, and rumors about future concert dates. Several of the fan sites indicated that they were part of a Web ring with even more fan sites—what was a fan to do with so much stuff?

I found myself every day running through a half-dozen music and political sites, looking for new stories, audio clips, and poll results. Yet once a day wasn't enough—I noticed that most of the sites were updated several times a day, and I felt compelled to go back. Whenever I felt writer's block hitting me, I'd head straight to the Web for a little escape. I would plan to get just five minutes worth of updates, then would find myself wasting an hour or two.

The Time Vacuum

After awhile I realized that the Internet makes time management difficult because it changes the way we perceive time.

Web sites or chat rooms don't place large clocks up in the corner of the screen to let you know how long you've been on-line. Unlike television, your favorite Internet material is not slated to be available at a set time of night and limited to a half-hour or one-hour block. Instead, Internet use can roll on for hours without any indications that time has elapsed.

Mike always seemed to lose track of time when he was on-line. "Time had no meaning to me," he recalls. Yet Mike also noticed another wrinkle in Internet time: around-the-clock activity. He had a problem with insomnia, and when he couldn't sleep he would get on the Internet and go into a chat room or play a game. "I'd be playing with someone in Sweden who was taking a break from work," he said. "Sometimes I would get to bed at four and have to be up at six."

Despite all the hype about instant communication on the Internet, I have noticed that one of the biggest time wasters is the amount of downtime I experience while trying to get all that "information at my fingertips." Nothing ever seems instant to me. Every search seems to return off-the-wall results, leading me on wild goose chases. Often the Web site with the information I want requires me to take time to register with them or to download required software. These delays are bad enough when the Internet is moving quickly; if I want something on a popular Web site, I may have to wait longer, especially when I'm using my slower connection at home. To top it all off, it seems that whenever I finally land on the exact piece of information I want, get my registration right, download the appropriate software, and wait for a good connection to the Web host, my browser will tell me that it has to shut down because I've performed some kind of "illegal operation." Internet hype promises information at the click of a mouse, but too often the experience is like a mouse lost in a maze—killing precious time with little to show for it.

Virtual Communities

Not surprisingly, the most popular applications of the Internet are relational in nature. Email, newsgroups, bulletin boards, instant messaging services, and multiplayer games all go beyond static content and give people an opportunity to interact with each other. For all the attention focused on the World Wide Web, email is the most frequently used Internet application. "I'm addicted to email," says a friend of mine named Kevin. "I have four email accounts and I compulsively check them throughout the day." While out of town for a convention, Kevin grew so anxious to check his email that he slipped out to a Kinko's and handed over his credit card for a few minutes of access to his email account.[1]

When it comes to on-line entertainment, however, chat

rooms rank near the top—or at least that's where they appeared in a recent survey by Cyber Dialogue.[2]

For a while Mike wandered around a variety of newsgroups, but it wasn't until he got into chat rooms that he really felt hooked. "My first experience with chat rooms was very disappointing," he says. "It was so dumb, so inane. The conversations were silly—just people saying things like, 'Hiya, how's everybody doing?' The grammar was bad and no one seemed to be finishing their sentences. I thought, 'What's the appeal? Why do people waste their time here?' I didn't bother trying chat rooms again for another month."

"My second experience, however, was very good. I went into a Christian chat room called 'Fellowship.' There were only two or three people in the room and they immediately recognized my presence. I introduced myself and asked about the other participants. Pretty soon, I felt like I was getting to know these people. I knew what part of the country they were from, what denomination they belonged to. The conversation was just like sitting in a room talking to a bunch of Christians. It was fun."

Mike was a pretty social guy before he went on-line, but he admits that his chat friends had an additional appeal. "There was a little novelty and mystery to it—meeting people you don't know and talking about interesting things. These people seemed more real and more important than the people around me."

Yet just how real and important can on-line relationships become? At the end of the day, long-distance, faceless relationships do not offer the kind of assistance and the sense of give-and-take needed for a fulfilling relationship. A recent study of Internet users by Carnegie Mellon University indicates that on-line relationships seldom bring the kind of "psychological security and happiness" that come from simple things like being available to baby-sit on a moment's notice or being able to get together for a cup of coffee. "Our hypothesis is there are more cases where you're building shallow relationships, leading to an overall decline in feeling of connection to other people," says Robert Kraut, a social psychology professor at Carnegie Mellon.[3]

"Those who celebrate 'virtual communities' created on-line forget that it takes more than shared interests to create a real community," said Chuck Colson on his radio broadcast, *Breakpoint.* "It requires the kind of proximity and everyday contact that enables your neighbors' concerns to become your own. Real-life friendships require transparency and openness in our dealings with one another."[4]

The Escape

"I got that 'Cheers' feeling in the Christian chat room," says Mike, "as if I was going to a place where everybody knew my name." That seems to be the experience a lot of people are looking for when they go on-line. I heard it said once, "we don't live in cities, we live in neighborhoods." In other words, when we are in large places, we have a way of gravitating to the people and places that are closest to us. Well, the vast universe of networked computers we know as the Internet is a very large place, and it's not surprising that out of the millions of Web sites they could visit, or the thousands of community areas (chat rooms, message boards, and newsgroups), people often settle in to something like a little neighborhood, with their favorite Web sites and communities.

Look at your favorite on-line bookmarks or think about the communities in which you spend the most time. Maybe, like

Mike, you have a place where "everybody knows your name"—even if it's not a real name. Maybe it's an on-line game that levels the playing field and gives you a chance to feel competitive and effective. Maybe it's a news site that rewards your every visit with new information and insight.

That little world—especially interactive community areas—can offer novelty and community, encouragement and security. Yet that place can also become an escape hatch—a place more attractive and easier to control than the unpredictable world around you, offering simpler relationships, acceptance without expectations, and gratification without delay.

Dr. Kimberly Young pioneered the study of abusive Internet use. "I've found that some form of escape usually lies at the heart and soul of the drive toward Internet addiction," she says.[5] Based on her surveys of compulsive users she compiled the following list of the most common things people try to escape while on-line:

1. Loneliness
2. Marital discontent
3. Work-related stress
4. Boredom
5. Depression
6. Financial problems
7. Insecurity about physical appearance
8. Anxiety
9. Struggles with recovery from other addictions
10. Limited social life[6]

"The downside, however, is that the escape is temporary," Young explains. "When the Internet addict finally logs off for the night, the screen goes dark on the fantasy world. Real-life problems return, and now they're even harder to endure."7

Obviously, the Internet isn't the first place to which people have turned for escape. For years, we've gone home and clicked on the television or lost ourselves in music or video games. Yet the Internet seems different—it seems to deliver an escape that is deeper, more complete.

For some, the experience of tapping on a computer mouse begins to feel ominously similar to the experience of a laboratory mouse tapping on a lever to make a treat appear. The urge begins to dominate their lives. Instead of bringing peace, it creates anxiety. Their nerves get tight if something stands between them and their favorite Internet experience. When they see it taking control, they often feel guilty for accepting a substitute or for cheating the people around them.

That feeling—the anticipation, the dependency, and the attachment—is a lot like addiction. Can you see addictive elements in your general Internet use? Have you lost the ability to limit yourself to reasonable blocks of time on-line? Do you compulsively check your email throughout the day? Do you hang out in an on-line place where everyone knows your name to the point that you are starting to forget the names of the people around you?

Internet use, no matter how innocent it may seem, can become addictive and push you beyond a balanced life. Taking the steps outlined in the last half of this book can help you to limit what you do on-line to an experience that enhances your life without dominating it.

Chapter Three

The Internet and Money Compulsions

Everyone loves to get a great bargain—to pay a lot less for something than it's worth or to sell something for more than it cost. We generally like the idea of easy money, also—scoring riches with little effort or investment. Yet the hunt for the great bargain or easy dollars can become an obsession, especially when the hunt is woven into a drive for power or control.

Millions of Americans already struggle with compulsive gambling habits or even compulsive shopping disorders, where their preoccupations directly interfere with their relationships, mental health, and financial well-being. The convenience and hyperspeed of the Internet seem to accelerate this problem in two ways: first by ratcheting up preexisting compulsions and second by lowering barriers that previously had kept others from developing compulsions.

Dr. David Greenfield describes such problems as "Internet-enabled addictions"—where a neutral medium facilitates a compulsive disorder. Dr. Kimberly Young combines compulsive on-line auctioning, gambling, and trading into a unique category of on-line addictions she labels "net compulsions." She explains that in each of these areas, users are motivated by feelings of power and self-esteem. "The ability to take control over one's own investing and the ability to purchase practically anything on the Web," she says, "has created a competitive climate for users that further perpetuates the bidder's, investor's, or shopper's Internet compulsion."[1]

Let's look at those categories as well as the emerging problem of compulsive on-line shopping.

Shopping

During the 1998 Christmas holidays, new creatures called "e-tailers" started barraging Americans with promises of exciting shopping opportunities on-line. They introduced shoppers to the convenience of browsing through thousands of products and never having to leave their house or stand in long lines.

A *U.S. News* story recently described the growth of on-line shopping and specifically detailed how Web marketers use customization features to make targeted sales pitches. For instance, after setting up an account at Amazon.com, I returned to find the following message at the top of the Amazon Web site: "Hello, Stephen O. Watters. We have <u>recommendations</u> for you in <u>Books</u>, <u>Music</u>, and <u>more</u>." *The U.S. News* writer warns, "The greatest danger may well be that personalization will work so well that shopping addiction becomes one of the first social problems of the 21st century."[2]

General on-line shopping may grow into an addictive problem soon, but it does not appear to be substantial at this time. Perhaps would-be on-line shopping addicts have been deterred by problems including poor customer service, botched deliveries, and credit card security concerns. Clifford Stoll, an Internet skeptic, believes on-line shopping will never quite compare to the experience of off-line shopping. "No electronic shopping can compare with the variety, quality, and experiential richness of a visit to even the most mundane malls," he says.[3]

I asked Dr. Young if she thought general shopping addiction is currently a problem. She hadn't seen evidence that it is. Surprisingly, several of the complaints she has heard have come from women. "I have wives concerned about all the packages coming to the house, purchased by their husbands." Young thinks this has more to do with men's general distaste for the headaches of the mall than it does with some kind of addiction problem.

Young sees this as more of an annoyance than an addiction— something couples will have to work through in terms of setting up appropriate spending limits and computer boundaries.[4]

Auctions

"What QVC did for cubic zirconia, eBay is doing for the junk in your attic," says a writer for the *Boston Herald*. The world's most popular virtual auction site, eBay is a yard sale, flea market, and antique store rolled into one and then multiplied by a thousand. Initiated as a Web site for collectors of Pez dispensers, eBay has revolutionized the auction market. Today, eBay competes alongside hundreds of other on-line auction sites with names like uBid, FirstAuction, and Haggle. In recent years, Yahoo, Microsoft, and Dell have jumped into the fray with their own auction services.[5]

U.S. users traded an estimated $1.3 trillion worth of goods on-line last year.[6] On-line auction services have breathed new life into the antiques and collectibles business. Many vendors have closed up their physical stores and now operate exclusively via virtual auction sites, where they benefit from a worldwide, around-the-clock market.

I remember the rush of my first on-line auction purchase. I

had recently attended the Pikes Peak Rodeo here in Colorado Springs and it made me think of the song "Rodeo" by Garth Brooks. I got on-line soon after I returned from the rodeo and tried to find some of the Garth Brooks music that was now nearly impossible to get out of my head. I visited Amazon.com first. They wanted $14.49 for the Garth Brooks CD I wanted. That seemed like a reasonable price to me, but then I noticed that it was out of stock.

I decided to check eBay. Within seconds of typing in the words "Garth Brooks," I struck gold. Not only was someone willing to part with their old cassette copy of the self-titled *Garth Brooks*, but they were throwing in a copy of *Ropin' the Wind* as well—and the highest bid to date was only $1.99. I noticed that the auction was coming quickly to a close, so I had to act fast. I rushed to sign up as a bidder. I eagerly awaited an email confirmation from eBay that would allow me to jump into the auction. With only a few hours to spare, I entered my bid of $4.99. I figured that amount might be high, but it was still a bargain compared to what I had been about to pay for the music.

Feeling motivated by my potential bargain, I placed another bid—for Garth Brook's *No Fences* CD. After an anxious wait, I found out that I had won both of my bids and I didn't even have to pay the full amount I had offered. All told, I got two cassettes and one CD in good condition for $3.50.

Then I had a thought that must cross the minds of many other on-line auction users: "If I had a need for someone else's junk, surely someone out there among the millions of auction shoppers will have a need for my junk." I seriously contemplated taking pictures of numerous items in my basement and placing them on eBay.

In a short time, I discovered the lure of bargains and sales opportunities that attracts millions of users to on-line auction sites ... including a small percentage who just can't get enough.

Erik Hedegaard was one of those people, and he told the long, sordid story about how he moved from eBay seller to eBay buyer and then to eBay addict in *Worth* magazine. He had had much more junk to sell than I did. His wife asked him to get rid of a whole slew of dishes, furniture, knickknacks, and other assorted goods that had been passed down from deceased relatives. He headed to eBay. Instead of taking a gamble with his own stuff first, however, he went to the Salvation Army and bought an old typewriter for $6 to try to sell. By writing up an auction notice filled with what he described as a lot of "Madison-Avenue-type huck," he was able to sell the typewriter for the absurd price of $232.56. He was hooked.

For the next several months, he tried to sell not only the junk in his own house, but also a growing collection of junk that he found at local garage sales, flea markets, and thrift shops. "After awhile I couldn't get enough of eBay," he writes. "It was a wonderful world, and I sunk into it completely. I loved getting up in the morning and seeing if anyone had bid on one of my auctions, and I loved doing that in the middle of the night, too. I loved hearing the clatter of mail dropping into my mailbox and finding it full of money, paying for goods that had cost me basically zilch."

Eventually, Erik began to devote more time and energy to on-line auctions than he did to his real job—even starting a little side business auctioning items for friends. It was starting to drive his wife and daughter crazy. He didn't care. "It didn't seem important to me," he said. "What was important to me was the peace I felt when I was inside eBay, inside a new world of mercantilism. I was somebody there, a presence, a force in a community."

Now he sees eBay as a substance as addictive as alcohol or tobacco. "It feels good, but it's bad," he says. "You start on it, thinking maybe you can clear your house of [junk], then all of a sudden you're hooked; you never do accomplish your original goal ... it possesses you. It messes with your finances, your marriage, and your kid's happiness.... And it's such a new drug that very few people are talking about how dangerous it can be."[7]

Dr. Kimberly Young compares on-line auction addiction to pathological gambling. "The auction method satisfies the addict's need for control and provides immediate gratification," she says. "The high of bidding brings the addict back, and the cycle repeats itself. It's the excitement of winning the prize. People want the rush."

Maybe your use of on-line auction sites has gotten out of control. Has the belief that you could land the best deal ever or turn your junk into riches motivated you to spend inordinate amounts of time at an auction site? Do you constantly check your email for updates on bids or obsess about buyer feedback comments? Do you find yourself browsing and bidding on auction items not because you want anything in particular but because you just enjoy your time on the auction site or think that you can resell an item for more money later?

If you recognize a problem, this is the time to begin to moderate your use of auction sites. You can find practical steps to do that in the last few chapters of this book.

Day-Trading

"Today for the first time ever, half of all American households own stock," said a recent *Wall Street Journal* article that described investing as the new national pastime. "Buying and selling stocks has become a staple of life, alongside work, family, and religion."[8]

People seem to like opportunities to make a lot of money off a minimal investment, and the high-rolling stock market of the past decade appears to be the preferred place to do that. Of course, the medium of choice for investing is the Internet. The Internet not only helped to create much of the new wealth, it became the place people wanted to go to make their investments and manage their wealth.

"Fire your broker," a popular ad encouraged last year, and a lot of people did. They quit bothering to dress up and drive to visit with a stockbroker to talk about investing. They didn't even bother to pick up the phone.

Why should they? The commercials told them they were the boss. They could get on-line, find all the investing information they needed, and then go make their own trades. They had the power, or, according to a letter I received in the mail from the trading service Datek Online, it was their "right."

"Dear Steve," the letter said, "Serious investors have rights. The rights to free, real-time streaming quotes that continuously update. The right to have your marketable on-line order executed within sixty seconds—or it's commission-free. The right to a twelve-hour trading day. In short, the right to access the power of professional trading tools once reserved for Wall Street insiders." Apparently, even I could join the more than four million others who have set up on-line accounts.

Being your own boss, however, can have a downside. "I have seen many men fall into the pattern commonly referred to as problem stock watching," says Dr. Young. She explains that people who take control of their own financial destiny begin to pay more attention to it—often watching their stocks on a daily basis and tracking "every dip and peak in the market."

"Attending to each fluctuation in the market, one becomes more emotional about investments," she says. "And with the volatility of the stock market, this can mean intense periods of anxiety and panic with each financial loss."[9]

That anxiety is an occupational hazard for a new kind of investor—the day-trader. According to investing columnist Humberto Cruz, day-trading is "the practice of buying and selling a stock in the same day—or quite often in a matter of hours, if not minutes—to profit from the tiniest movement in the stock's price."

Day-traders often work independently, without managers or supervisors who could manage trading, share strategy, and provide safeguards against greediness and addiction. Cruz says that, despite all the magazine articles that glamorize it, day-trading is a bad way to pursue wealth. "Day-trading is the bastardization of on-line investing, a dangerous addiction that can ruin you."

Cruz is disappointed that so many voices in today's financial culture place the emphasis on "trading" instead of on "investing." "When you invest in stocks," he says, "you put your money in companies you believe will prosper over time. If you're right, you'll share in the company's growth and profits. When you day-trade, stocks are just chips in a casino game."[10]

Day-trading is frequently compared to gambling. Arnie Wexler is a recovering gambler who travels the country addressing gambling addiction. When I called to ask him about Internet gambling, he wanted to tell me about all the people he had met with day-trading problems. Like the guy he met at a wedding. He was a retired professional who had started day-trading his 401K and lost $400,000 in one year.

Or the thirty-nine-year-old who retired from business and then got into on-line trading because of something he heard in a chat room. He started with $475,000 and lost all but $25,000 of it.

Or the friend who took out an equity loan for $100,000 and started playing the stock market. He paid the loan up for six months, so his wife wouldn't get any notices in the mail. He started trading on-line at night and during the day from his job. He finally had to fess up when he blew all the money.

The chances of making a lot of money day-trading just aren't that good. The Financial Services Authority emphasizes that only 11 percent of all day-traders make money, while 70 percent of them lose big—often real big.[11] "You have better chances going to a casino with a blindfold over your eyes and throwing craps on the table."[12] Losses are even larger when traders are using borrowed money (trading on margin). Not surprisingly, there is a high dropout rate among day-traders.[13]

The only people who win at day-trading are the on-line brokerage services that lure inexperienced investors into the habit and then collect fifteen to twenty-five dollars in brokerage fees on every rapid-fire trade they encourage. "Day-trading is clearly a gamble for most traders, but certainly not for the day-trading firms," said Senator Susan Collins after an eight-month investigation of the practice. "[The firms] make money whether their customers do or not." She hoped her congressional hearings on the subject would make the public more aware of the risks of this form of trading.[14]

Addicts of all stripes typically deny that they have a problem, but day-traders can have greater difficulty with denial because what they are doing is associated with a legitimate business. "Most of the people don't see it as a gambling problem," says Edward Looney, executive director of the Council on Compulsive Gambling. "They just see it as bad decisions that they made on the market. They are gambling, and they just don't see it."[15]

Many don't see it because day-trading seems to have a certain hipness to it. Unlike gambling, it doesn't usually have a negative stigma. A friend of mine, Marcus Tovar, lost money trading on-line but helped me understand the attraction to day-trading. "If you're at a party and someone mentions that they have just earned $10,000 trading on-line," he said, "They get a much warmer response than if they had just said, 'I just won $10,000 at the blackjack table.'"[16]

A tragic event in the summer of 1999 exposed the nightmare side of day-trading. For fifteen days Mark Barton watched his losses pile up, until he had lost $105,000 day-trading. Then he lost it all together. He drove over to two companies with which he had been trading and killed twelve people before killing himself. Later reports have indicated that Barton clearly had some other problems, yet the dramatic day-trading loss seemed to be the real trigger.[17]

Shortly after that tragedy, Arthur Levitt, then chairman of the Securities and Exchange Commission, appeared before Senator Collins' Senate committee. "I am concerned," he said, "that some day-traders don't fully understand the risk they are assuming. I am concerned that some people may be lured into the false belief that day-trading is a surefire strategy to make them rich." Levitt went on to stress the need for on-line brokerage services to fully disclose risks up front to customers and to "screen potential day-traders to determine suitability."[18]

Even with safeguards in place, day-trading can be a highly addictive and risky approach to making money. Dr. Young has seen clients lose homes, jobs, and marriages due to day-trading. She says the traders often became "extremely depressed and even suicidal with each rapid market drop."[19]

If you are spending a lot of time anxiously following stocks on-line, you should take steps to moderate your on-line investment activity. If you fit the category of a day-trader, you need to recognize the seriousness of the risk you have undertaken and break away from this addictive approach to pursuing wealth.

Gambling

"I have control of my gambling behavior, but the presence of gambling on the Internet made it uncontrollable," an anonymous addict told the Congressional committee considering a bill to ban Internet gambling. Speaking under the name "John Doe," the gentleman explained that he grew up in Las Vegas and enjoyed the gambling scene. Yet it was not until he saw a banner ad promoting an on-line casino that he developed a serious problem.

"I'll have to admit that gambling for real money from the luxury and comfort of my own home was quite an exhilarating rush," he said. "The first time I gambled on-line I won $400. I thought to myself, 'I just made $400 in two hours and didn't even have to leave the house to do it!'" Eventually, he started using his dad's credit card to gamble. He was supposed to use it only for emergencies, but with a $5,000 limit, he saw it as his chance to make some big money.

"It's as if the computer was calling me to go to it and play blackjack," he said. "It all went downhill from this point. It was just too easy to do, and I couldn't stop. It got so bad that when I had friends over, I would sometimes hope they would leave soon so I could indulge myself in this masochistic behavior in privacy once again." In only three weeks, "John" maxed out his dad's credit card. "I was severely depressed, nervous, and suicidal [after that]," he said.[20]

Twenty years ago, legalized gambling operated in only two states, Nevada and New Jersey. Today, it operates in some form in all but two states. No longer do Americans have to fly to Las Vegas or Atlantic City to lose their money. Most Americans now live within a few hours' drive of some form of gambling—a riverboat casino, a horse or dog track, video poker machines, or Native American casinos. Over half of the states now have Las Vegas casino-style gambling.

A recent federal commission on gambling estimated that 125 million American adults now gamble in one form or another. That's over half of our adult population. No wonder Americans spend more money on gambling than they do on movies, spectator sports, concerts, CDs, theme parks, video games, and even cruise ships combined.[21]

The federal commission explained that 15.4 million Americans fall into the categories of problem and pathological gamblers. Research they commissioned indicates that pathological gamblers, "engage in destructive behaviors: they commit crimes, they run up large debts, they damage relationships with family and friends, and they kill themselves." The commission gave an ominous warning: "With the increased availability of gambling and new gambling technologies, pathological gambling has the potential to become even more widespread."[22]

That's where the Internet comes in—closing any remaining availability gap and conveniently delivering gambling to everyone. Arnie Wexler struggled with old-fashioned casinos. "Now, we've allowed the Internet to put casinos in offices, college dorms, and homes," he says. "Anyone can play anywhere, at anytime." An Internet connection and a credit card are usually all you need to gamble in almost any form—poker, blackjack, roulette, slot machines, and more—around the clock, without leaving your desk.

Arnie set up a Web site to reach people who can't stay out of the casinos. One lady wrote to describe the mess she was able to get into from home. "I got hooked in by an innocent email message which contained a hypertext link to an on-line casino," she said, "After three days, hardly any sleep, and my credit card right next to my computer, I had lost $6,000."

Internet casinos handled $2.2 billion in 2000, according to Christiansen Capital Advisors. A filtering service called Websense recorded a 169 percent increase in the number of gambling Web sites in a six-month period alone last year.[23]

Four million Americans are currently gambling on-line, according to Cyber Dialogue research service.[24] That number could grow substantially, however, if the United States Congress caves in to pressure to repeal its ban on illegal gambling. Currently, the majority of on-line gambling sites are run out of Romania, or Antigua in the Caribbean.

"If gambling in general is a dumb bet, then gambling on the Internet is a very dumb bet," says James Doyle, head of the National Association of Attorneys General.[25] While some casinos make an effort to watch for compulsive gamblers and try to keep them from getting out of control, the Internet doesn't have that level of accountability. "A compulsive user can rack up thousands of dollars in debt without anyone knowing," explains Dr. Valerie Lorenz, executive director of the Compulsive Gambling Center in Baltimore. "There's no one around who can regulate the gambler or put a stop to it, and there's often not a limit to how much money you can wager."[26]

In fact, the user may not even be an adult. It could be a teenager who wants to bet on sports and has grabbed his parents' credit card. "As the Internet reaches more and more schoolchildren, Internet gambling is certain to promote even more gambling among young people," Jeff Pash, executive vice president of the NFL, told the Senate Judiciary Committee. "Because no one stands at the door to the virtual casino checking IDs, our children have the means to gamble on the computer after school."[27]

Not surprisingly, on-line gambling is exploding on college campuses. College students have free time and free Internet access, and often have multiple credit cards—making them a perfect market for on-line gambling. In fact, one offshore gambling site conducted a marketing study that identified college-age students as a significant demographic target.[28]

"Internet gambling is as dangerous as alcohol on campuses," says Andy Lissak. "Colleges just don't realize how bad it is." Andy saw an ad for an Internet gambling service in his West Virginia University school paper. He checked the site out and spun out of control in a quick period of time. He started going on-line to place sports bets as often as three times a day. His obsession came back to bite him as his grades dropped sharply, he lost his girlfriend, and he racked up $7,000 in credit card debt.[29]

A lady called Arnie Wexler last year. She told him that her son was in the early years of college. He had never gambled before, but he started betting on-line. In a short time, he lost over $30,000 from a checking account and a credit card.

"It is easier today for a kid on a college campus to place a bet than it is to buy a can of beer or a pack of cigarettes," says Wexler.[30]

It should come as no surprise that Internet gambling is now a substantial problem among teens and college students. For most of their lives they have watched gambling expand around them. They've either seen new facilities go up in their states or watched endless commercials where the gambling industry or even the state government touted the benefits of lotteries and casinos. After hearing such tremendous spin from the industry and seeing the industry embraced by the government, this new generation is less likely to see gambling as a vice or sin that should be avoided.

Some Christians have argued that "thou shall not gamble" didn't make it into the Ten Commandments in the Bible and therefore gambling is not a sin. "In actuality," says Ron Reno, "there is a multitude of scriptural principles that bear directly on how Christians should view this activity." As a gambling research analyst, Ron served as a key assistant to Dr. James Dobson during his service on the National Gambling Impact Study Commission.

He drafted a brief called "Gambling and the Bible" after hearing from numerous Christians who felt gambling wasn't a big deal. The first point he makes is that "gambling is predicated on the losses, pain, and suffering of others," and therefore violates Christ's command to "Love your neighbor as yourself" (Mk 12:31). He goes on to demonstrate how gambling exploits the poor, whom we are supposed to protect, and how it undermines the stewardship and work ethic expected of believers. Most importantly, gambling is founded on greed and indicates a lack of trust in God's provisions.

Have you placed a bet on-line? Have you tried to hide an Internet gambling habit from family and friends? Do you obsess about betting opportunities when you are away from the Internet? Gambling is a problem, and for the Christian, the only option is abstinence.

The convenience and excitement of gambling sites, day-trading services, and even auction sites can bring out the worst in someone who already has a compulsive money problem. It can also spur addictive behavior in someone who didn't think they had a money problem before. If any of these descriptions fit you, for the stability of your finances, relationships, and peace of mind, you need to take steps to break free from compulsive Net behavior today.

Chapter Four

Games

In 1972, a new company called Atari chose Andy Capp's Cavern, a bar in Sunnyvale, California, for a little experiment. They mounted onto pinball bars a prototype of the first Pong arcade machine and waited to see the reaction. Here's how it was captured in the book *The Rise and Fall of Atari:*

> One of the regulars approached the Pong game inquisitively and studied the ball bouncing silently around the screen as if in a vacuum. A friend joined him. The instructions said: "Avoid missing ball for high score." One of [them] inserted a quarter. There was a beep. The game had begun. They watched dumbfounded as the ball appeared alternately on one side of the screen and then disappeared on the other. Each time it did the score changed. The score was tied at 3-3 when one player tried the knob controlling the paddle at his end of the screen. The score was 5-4, his favor, when his paddle made contact with the ball. There was a beautifully resonant "pong" sound, and the ball bounced back to the other side of the screen. 6-4. At 8-4 the second player figured out how to use his paddle. They had their first brief volley just before the score was 11-5 and the game was over.
>
> Seven quarters later they were having extended volleys, and the constant pong noise was attracting the curiosity of others at the bar. Before closing, everybody in the bar had played the game. The next day people

were lined up outside Andy Capp's at 10 A.M. to play Pong.[1]

From the beginning, it seems, video games have been addictive. Whether they are guided by knobs, buttons, joysticks, or a computer mouse, video games have beckoned users to escape into fantasy worlds populated by race cars, tanks, spaceships, mythical creatures, and more for the past thirty years.

In that time, however, two trends emerged and then, recently, converged. First, a significant number of video games evolved beyond the arcade and the cartridge system and onto the personal computer. Second, early adapters of what became the Internet took breaks from defense and research work to create games that could be played by individuals or by several users across the network.

Today, nearly twenty million on-line gamers choose diversions ranging from virtual card and board games to intricately layered and detailed role-playing games.[2] Surprisingly, most of those gamers are not kids. Ninety percent of video and computer games sold in the United States are, in fact, bought by adults.[3] Mike, an adult player, loved the fact that he could go on-line any time and find someone who wanted to play Scrabble, Monopoly, Yahtzee, cribbage, or whatever he was in the mood for. "The players on-line provided better competition and were more available than anyone I could find in real life," he said.

Play for Pay

Most of the big Web portals like Yahoo!, Lycos, or Alta Vista provide a launching pad to the array of on-line games, but several sites create their own little universe of games with built-in incentives to play on their site. Take Sandbox.com for example.

"For 3.5 million guys, we're better than porn," the magazine ad said. "Not one hot, naked female and still Sandbox.com is one of the ten most addictive sites on the Web."⁴ Sandbox membership had grown to 4.8 million by the time I checked out the site, and I could tell why: it is addictive. It hosts over fifty free games, including trivia, sweepstakes, fantasy sports, arcade, and what it calls "play-for-fun casino" games. Yet the big lure for Sandbox.com is what I call the "Chuck E. Cheese effect." Remember going to Chuck E. Cheese and racing through your pizza so that you could go play all those games that paid out in perforated carnival tickets? The incentive, of course, was to get tons of tickets so that you could redeem them for big prizes at the counter later.

Sandbox offers the grown-up version of that: a currency they call sand dollars—earnable throughout their site and redeemable for "hot products, gift certificates, and promotional offers from a variety of merchant partners." For instance, the offer of the day when I visited was a digital phone, valued at $188 but available to the Sandbox member by signing up for the "AT&T Digital Advantage 400 Plan" and cashing in ten thousand "sand dollars." To earn those sand dollars, members could play tons of games, or they could earn quick dollars by paying for services ranging from on-line flowers to magazine subscriptions and travel packages.

Sandbox has plenty of competition. In a quick search for more, I found _Z-Games_, who promised me I could get paid for playing on-line games; _GameMachine_, offering "cash prizes up to a million dollars!"; and _CashWars_, described as "An online game where users can steal real money from other people, ally with friends, win great prizes, and build an empire."

Another site, FantasyGamez, focuses specifically on the popular fantasy football, baseball, basketball, hockey, golf, and

NASCAR leagues. Fantasy sports can be rather consuming to begin with, but FantasyGamez goes a step further by offering prizes, "from T-shirts, PalmPilots, TVs, Computers, Entertainment Systems, all the way up to a cool $1,000,000 in cash!"

The Great Escape

At first glance, it's easy to see all the on-line gaming as, well, fun and games. Very few on-line games appear harmful on the surface. While sex and violence show up in some, most seem innocuous. Yet that's not where the core problem lies. "The real danger of video games isn't the amount of violent or other questionable content," says Walter Park, a designer for Saffire Video Game Developer, "but the escape it provides from a real life to a fantasy world."[5]

Dr. Maressa Orzack specializes in treating gamers who have gone overboard. One of her patients was a recovering drug addict who told her that video games gave him "a high like any amphetamine."[6]

Compulsive game playing seems to be acute on college campuses. At least 10 percent of college students have a problem with their Internet use, says Dr. Keith J. Anderson, a psychologist at Rensselaer Polytechnic Institute. He insists that the majority is male.[7]

Dr. Kimberly Young noticed in her research that men were more frequently drawn to interactive on-line games than women, and that they seemed to enjoy the feeling of power associated with moving up in ranks and gaining strength and status with playing time. "Not only is status achieved through these games," she says, "but more often men seek to dominate other players as characters have the power to blow up, stab, shoot, and kill other players in a game."[8]

Women are definitely playing on-line as well, however. Cyber Dialogue surprised many trend watchers in a recent survey showing that 47 percent of on-line gamers are female.[9] Stacey Frokovich, a veteran gamer, says she likes to "kick butt along with the men." Even though women aren't as aggressively targeted by video game vendors as men are, Web sites such as WomenGamers and United Female Gamers Kingdom indicate that a substantial female audience is playing on-line games.[10]

Perhaps female players are more aware of the addictive nature of on-line games. I found a tongue-in-cheek game addiction Web site hosted by a guy, but it wasn't until I visited the WomenGamers site that I found a meaningful article about on-line gaming addiction.

"Computer games are specifically created to be immersive and addictive: just one more hour, one more level, one more match," says the writer. "In the computer gaming scene, the word 'addiction' is ubiquitous, as gamers joke about their obsessions with certain games." She goes on to explain that fixation with a game is the occupational hazard of being a gamer, pointing out that "sleep deprivation is almost expected in hardcore gaming circles when new games come out."[11]

In a quick review of recent news stories on Internet game problems, I found examples of several women who struggled. One woman played cribbage, backgammon, and spades on-line up to twenty hours at a time—losing friends and a husband in the process. On-line games drove Sandra Hacker of Cincinnati to ignore her family up until police finally arrested her for inadequately caring for her children, who were found sitting in a playroom filled with broken glass, debris, and even handprints in human excrement on the walls.[12]

Stuck in the MUD

"I was drawn to this alternate reality," says Mark, who was a student at a Christian college at the time. "I'd be sitting in the computer lab clicking away but I would be off in a different realm." His alternate reality was a MUD, or multi-user domain, one of the most addictive formats for on-line games.

"A MUD is an elaborate, computer-mediated, imaginary environment," Harley Hahn explains in his "Guide to MUDs." "Most muds are designed around a general theme, for example fantasy, medieval, sci-fi, cyberpunk, gothic or post-apocalypse."[13]

During the summer after his freshmen year in college, a friend introduced Mark to MUDs. The two would go to a university computer lab a couple of times a week and play for an hour or so. By the time Mark returned to college he was ready to play more. Using telnet on the college network, he started playing Jedi MUD—a game he was drawn to as a Star Wars fan.

He described the game as a "hack and slash," meaning that he needed to kill computer-generated creatures to advance. He would fight them to earn gold coins, weapons, and new skills. His goal was to advance the player he created in equipment, experience, and strength. The game provided plenty of room to grow, with new areas and equipment added frequently and thirty levels to work his way through. The longer he played, the stronger he grew. To keep him coming back, the game subtracted points for every twenty-four hours he was away. Upon returning, he had to spend some of his coins to regain his status.

Mark soon got caught up in the rush of the game, finding it a great relief from the pressures of college. "I knew that my character would grow in power based on the number of hours I invested," he said, "and I found that this quest for power helped me escape from bad test results or anything that seemed out of my control." He also enjoyed how easy it was to build relationships. By being able to create his own identity and earn respect for his accomplishments, he never had to worry about his income, appearance, or circumstances the way he had to in real life.

Despite some ribbing from friends, Mark started mudding all the time. His first long stretch ran six hours. Once he stayed on campus during a break and spent the time playing around the clock, taking breaks only to eat and sleep. Eventually he ended up skipping some classes and homework. "I would say, 'I'll just play for an hour or so and then study,' but I wouldn't." He cut back on hanging out with friends, except for those who also played the games, and his conversations with them would be dominated by game activities and lingo. Sometimes they'd sit side by side in the computer lab and play together—each caught up in the faraway world.

Mark found himself thinking about the game continually. "I thought about the things I wanted to possess for my character," he said. "This happened when I was about to go to sleep, in class, or anytime I would daydream. Sometimes I'd think about it when I was trying to pray or think about spiritual things."

"I thought it might be a problem the whole time," says Mark, "but I didn't want to have to agree with my friends who complained about my use. Often I'd try to stop, but the computer was sitting there like a patient puppy dog ready to be played with."

Mark's experience is by no means uncommon for a "mudder." In fact, it almost seems modest compared to other typical players. For one thing, Mark never made it to a LAN (local area network) party, where groups of avid players connect their computers together for faster performance and then play through an entire weekend.

He also never bought or sold virtual game items on an auction site, like Greg Bachrach, who claims to make up to $3,000 a week playing a game called Ultima Online. Bachrach plays his favorite game around twenty hours a week and then posts items collected from the game for sale on eBay.[14] Believe it or not, people are willing to bid on imaginary gold, weapons, houses, and more on auction sites.

I found hundreds of gaming items listed on eBay along with the kind of sales pitches only a gamer could love. The seller of this character on Microsoft's Asheron's Call hopes to get a financial reimbursement for what he lost in his social life:

> *Asheron's Call Leafcull lvl60 ppGSA/GSA+more!* Mecrobe ... The level 60 Unarmed/Bow/Item/Life/Creature. What can I say? I know you are thinking, how fun could this character possibly be? Let's just say it has affected my social life. This character is extremely time consuming. He has met many people and he was ranked #5 for the highest Unarm Skill in Leafcull. There is nothing that can stop this extreme character.... *High bid $2,025.00*[15]

At first Richard Garriott was surprised that people found a way to make real money off his game Ultima Online. Now he plans to build the ability to sell virtual goods and services into his next game. "One of my primary design philosophies is to create a game mechanic so people can earn an income in the game, *quit their real jobs and live in the virtual world forever*" (italics added).[16] Now that's scary.

The Forever Quest

EverQuest stands high among competitors in the world of multiplayer on-line games. Sony claims that over 210,000 people have bought their game and now pay $9.95 a month to explore and conquer their virtual world on-line.[17]

Unlike some multiplayer games that are just text, EverQuest offers fifty levels of visually rich 3-D images filled with thousands of creatures, treasures, and adventures. The hook for EverQuest is that you can't quite beat it. "No matter how much you play, you can't ever really master it," says Helene Sheler, a PR person for the game's creator.[18]

Of course there are plenty of people who try to master it anyway, and the addictive draw has led some of them to rename the game "Evercrack."[19] "I know I am addicted. There is no doubt about it," says Veronica Randall, a thirty-four-year-old mother of four. "I have given up real-life activities. I have turned down offers with friends. I have spent thousands of dollars on computer equipment. I have had my children tell me they think the computer is more important to me than they are."[20]

"This game was so captivating ... there were actually times when I spent about thirty hours on-line," wrote an anonymous EverQuest player on Dr. David Greenfield's addiction Web site. "It's interesting that I could have become so immersed in this game which is basically just numbers and programmed code. I think the allures and dangers of addiction in this game and games like it lie in the fact that it satisfies many needs ... social interaction ... gratification that you receive when you accomplish quests and gain levels and items ... also the cheap entertainment factor."[21]

Recognizing a Problem

"Healing starts with recognizing and admitting there is a problem," wrote the anonymous EverQuest player on Dr. Greenfield's site. He entered his comments shortly after having a serious epiphany about the dangerous effects of his gaming addiction. "Three days ago at four in the morning I was lying awake in my bed, thinking, 'What am I doing and where is this leading?'" he wrote. "After some thought I realized I was compromising my future of having a nice job and earning a nice income. My soul literally shivered and my heart skipped a beat when I thought about the consequences of getting kicked out of school and wondering what I would do if I got kicked out [of my] profession. I got out of bed next and uninstalled the game from my computer and decided I was not going to play the game again for at least a month. One of the hardest things I had ever done."

Too often addicted gamers don't stop to think about their habit until they have flunked out of college, lost a job, or lost a marriage. Rene Roberts didn't see the extent of her problem until after her husband left her. As a last-ditch effort to save the marriage, a counselor encouraged her to "take the computer and throw it out the window," but she stayed on-line instead.[22]

You may be asking yourself, "When does recreational on-line gaming really become a compulsive problem?" The WomenGamers site explains that the gamer crosses the line when that person's playing affects other aspects of his or her life: "If your grades are slipping, if you've lost a job because of your preoccupation with gaming, if your partner complains of being a 'game widow,' if you're constantly tired from lack of sleep ... if you like yourself more as your RPG (role-playing game) character than in face-to-face interactions, you might want to take a look at the effect that your game playing is having on your life."[23]

Are you seeing any of these effects? Have you tried to conceal the amount of time you play on-line? Have computer crashes or other interruptions during gaming ever caused you to be angry? Have you found yourself incapable of cutting back on playing time? If so, you have a problem that may require outside help. You need to take steps to moderate your playing time, and you may need help to quit playing altogether.

Chapter Five

Relationships

"I feel very alone," said the email I received from Beth. "My husband and I were married eight years, very active in church, and I was a Sunday school teacher for years. I met a guy on-line, left my husband and left church abruptly with no explanation. I have not been to church since last June.... I am separated, living on my own. I have come to realize I am a sexual addict.... It is an embarrassing thing to admit. I am a college-educated career person. I can't believe I let Satan get a foothold in my life. I was at a peak in my spiritual walk when I fell. I am on the Internet all the time, waiting to meet the next guy. I know I need to get back into church and let go of this but I don't know if I am ready. Just messed up right now."

I could sense the desperation and disappointment in Beth's email. She couldn't believe how radically an on-line relationship had changed her life. The addictive nature had started to dominate her personality. "My whole world revolved around being home at a certain time so that I could get on-line," she said. "I would go nuts if I could not get on for some reason. I neglected housework, kids, everything to be on-line at times. If [the guy I was chatting with] was on-line and one of the kids was using the computer, I practically dragged them off kicking and screaming, not one of my proudest moments."

The worst part, however, was the affair. Beth's husband drove a truck and was gone a lot. He also had some difficulty communicating his feelings to Beth. In her loneliness, Beth visited a chat room. "The person I had the affair with was a Christian and that's how we started talking. We had long talks about religion, and I saw nothing wrong. It just escalated, and we drew closer and closer, always using the excuse that it was OK because we were both Christians—very weak Christians, I have come to find out. How sad."

Sad, but not isolated. Beth's story came to me among other tragic stories emailed to Pure Intimacy, a Web site I launched at Focus on the Family to address on-line sexual temptations. I notice in most of the stories I read a sense of surprise at how easily on-line relationships can grow addictive and adulterous.

Addictive Nature

When someone is fixated on achieving sexual pleasure to the point that they don't care if it causes hurt for themselves or the people around them, they have a sexual addiction. Sexual addictions are often tied to sexual abuse. Dr. Patrick Carnes estimates that more than 80 percent of sex addicts were sexually abused at some point in their lives.[1] An addiction to sex often shows up without the Internet, but after surveying hundreds of people who have had on-line relationships, Dr. Kimberly Young suggests that three factors—anonymity, convenience, and escape—can create an environment on-line that actually makes promiscuous and addictive behavior more likely.[2]

Anonymity

"Leave your inhibitions at the door," says the teaser for the Romance 101 club at the Excite portal—and that's what anonymity leads many to do. Behind the mask of digital communication, Internet users worry less about who they are. Faceless communication on the Internet helps people overcome shyness and awkwardness. Wallflowers can step into the spotlight. Those who are self-conscious about their body image can focus on the things they like best about themselves. Someone like Beth can slip into a chat room (or another interactive area) hidden behind a screen name like FunGirl and start to say bold things she would never say in public.

I remember making this discovery when I first went on-line in college. Too often I had stumbled through face-to-face conversations with girls I was eager to impress. Finally, I had the opportunity to plan my comments, to come up with ideas that I thought were humorous and notable. In email messages, I could even edit the words that were poorly chosen. Although I had to be quicker on my feet in chat rooms, I still didn't have to worry about what my nonverbals communicated. It didn't matter what I was wearing or even what might be hanging out of my nose.

Anonymity also allows men and women to indulge fantasies without worrying that their spouses will catch them. "Chat rooms provide women the opportunity to act out fantasies fueled by romance novels," says Marnie Ferree, a counselor specializing in female sex addiction.[3] Ferree points out that female sex addictions often are tied to intimacy disorders fueled by lack of nurture, as well as sexual abuse and trauma from past and present relationships. Lonely, unable to articulate her needs, a woman can be strongly drawn to anonymous communication.

"The distance afforded by cyberspace enables a person to share intimate feelings often reserved for a significant other," says Dr. Young, "thus opening the door for bonding and an accelerated sense of intimacy, which in turn can evolve into a cyberaffair or cybersex."[4]

I once received an email showing that pattern and demonstrating the danger of on-line anonymity. A girl, let's call her Jen, attended college in Colorado. Having recently broken up with her boyfriend, she found herself home alone on a Friday night for the first time in the three years they had been dating.

Feeling alone and depressed, she ventured over to a sexual chat line, where she met a guy who identified himself as "Jeremy." She introduced herself as "Katie" and started flirting sensually. He responded in kind, and the conversation heated up until it turned into cybersex.

She agreed to meet him again the following night. They become even closer that night, and kept it up for a week. The virtual relationship carried on like this for months, and the months turned into a year. By the end of the year they had exchanged their most intimate thoughts, but had never even spoken on the phone. Finally, the time came: they just had to meet each other. They didn't care about age or looks. They were in love. Jeremy told Jen he thought she could be his next wife. Jen was wary at first, but decided she didn't care how old or ugly he might be. She loved him, and he was the only one she could feel comfortable with. They planned to meet in Vail, Colorado.

Jen showed up at the resort first and checked in, telling the lady at the desk to hold a key for the next party. Then she headed to the room. Wanting things to be special, she lit a few candles and put on some music. She took off her clothes and climbed under the covers, deciding to surprise Jeremy when he got there.

The lights were out and the mood was perfect when she heard a key jiggling in the door. She heard someone walk in and around the corner. She whispered, "Jeremy?" A voice replied, "Katie?" "Yes," she said. He fumbled for the light, and turned it on to see Jen lying on the bed, naked. Two blood-curdling screams pierced the silence. Jen covered herself up and in her most humiliated voice said, "DAD?"

The email ends with the assurance that this story really happened. Then again, it's an anonymous email, very likely an urban myth. The power of urban myths, however, is the lesson they teach even if they aren't proven. The lesson of this story is that the mask of anonymity can make a relationship mysterious but also disastrous.

Convenience

Credit cards, drive-thru windows, 800-numbers, and home delivery all make shopping more convenient. Yet companies don't use these conveniences just to make life easier for their current shoppers; they also use them to attract new shoppers—people who might not have bought their product before because of inconvenience.

While many Internet users may have had an affair or a sexual addiction anyway, the Internet increases the likelihood that they will, simply by increasing convenience. In the past, the workplace and various social spots served as meeting places for people who wanted to form new relationships. Yet the need to go to a specific place at a specific time can be inconvenient. Even personal ads in newspapers and magazines require a certain amount of inconvenience.

The Internet streamlines the whole meeting process. Around the clock and around the world, on-line services can match people with like interests and set them up with a variety of formats for getting to know each other—bulletin boards, newsgroups, multiplayer games, chat rooms, email, instant messaging, and so forth. Because it all takes place on a computer, the user can move easily from a spreadsheet to spicy communication, at home or at work.

For that matter, any visitor to the most popular Web sites is only a click away from spicy communication. Yahoo!, Alta Vista, iVillage, and other popular Web entry points all tout their various clubs, boards, and chat areas. Many of the relationship-oriented areas on these sites are fairly mainstream—with names like "The Romance Connection," "Single Moms Looking for Men Who Won't Run," and so forth. Others throw out all subtlety: "Married and Attached Women Seeking MORE," "Swinging Couples," and worse. Dr. Young explains that areas like these, designed primarily for facilitating infidelity, "may intrigue a casual browser who is initially shocked, but at the same time titillated by the permissiveness of others engaged in virtual adultery."[5]

Soon, people who may never have gone through the effort to initiate a real-life affair find themselves sinking deeper and deeper into a virtual affair, perhaps even moving on to phone sex and arranged meetings. For others who have already had affairs or sexual addictions, the convenience of the Internet makes it tempting for them to fall back into old patterns. "In my experience, cybersex addiction comes from the ease at which a person who already has a sex addiction problem can access anything and everything sexual that one can imagine," wrote a fifty-eight-year-old man to Dr. Schneider. "It's convenient; you can go there twenty-four hours a day and stay for as long as you choose."[6]

Escape

For twelve years, Bob was a youth minister who worked for a Christian record company. When the company downsized and Bob lost his job, he felt despondent and headed to the chat rooms. "It was a Band-Aid of sorts that soothed the pain," he said. Pursuing that escape, however, he met a woman in a Christian chat room and started an affair that almost destroyed his marriage.

The elation of escape in on-line relationships can be intense. It's tempting to bypass the difficulties and disappointments of real-life relationships for the fantasy, the novelty, and the control of on-line relationships. "A lonely woman suddenly feels desired by her many cyberpartners, or a sexually insecure man transforms into a hot cyber lover that all the women in the chat room want," Dr. Young explains. "The experience not only provides sexual fulfillment, but allows a subjective mental escape achieved through the development of an on-line fantasy life where a person can adopt a new persona and on-line identity."[7]

The escape to a new on-line identity as well as the escape to a fantasy on-line partner is a direct attempt to fill a fundamental relational need, says Dr. Harry Schaumburg. He points out that from the beginning of time, men and women have longed to be known and loved deeply by each other.[8] Achieving that level of intimacy, however, became more difficult after the fall of Adam and Eve. Because we are all sinful and imperfect people, we will inevitably disappoint each other. That reality creates two strong temptations: one is to keep our own weaknesses hidden, and the second is to find a fantasy partner who doesn't appear to have weaknesses.

On-line meeting areas are perfect places to escape from a

flawed real-life identity and to find a fantasy partner. Behind the mask of anonymity, you can exaggerate all of your strengths and camouflage your weaknesses—and so can the person on the other end. Such a safe and exciting place can be hard to leave. Its brightness can make the workplace, housework, and friends and family look dull in comparison— leading to negligence and even abandonment.

"I ignore my family to talk on-line when they need me," a thirty-five-year-old married woman told Dr. Schneider. For two years the woman drifted away from her family while desperately looking for idealized romance on-line. "I want to be accepted and loved by someone who will be my 'knight in shining armor,'" she says. "I know that is not really going to happen, but I keep looking anyway.... I keep imagining that one day one of these men will really love me."[9]

When Is It Cheating?

For this woman, the allure of a "knight in shining armor" on-line pushed her over the line and into adultery. She arranged to meet several on-line lovers at hotels for sex. Yet when exactly did she cross the line? Did her relationship become adulterous when she had sex with another man, or did it begin as soon as she started flirting?

"Women often justify their on-line relationships because they see them as virtual, not adulterous," says Marnie Ferree, "especially if the relationship is only emotional, not sexual yet."[10] Women cross the line, however, as soon they begin to sneak around behind their husband's backs to share intimate thoughts with another man. "Stay-at-home moms in chat rooms are sharing all this personal stuff they are hiding from their partners," says Peggy Vaughan, America Online expert on problems caused by infidelity. She adds that such experiences can "quickly escalate into their thinking they have found a soul mate. It's so predictable, it is like a script."[11]

"[On-line relationships] can threaten marriages, even if there is no sex involved," says Dr. Shirley Glass, a Baltimore-based psychologist who has been studying infidelity for over twenty years. "Such on-line liaisons involve the three elements of an emotional affair: secrecy, intimacy, and sexual chemistry."[12]

Understandably, many participants in on-line communities never intended for their innocent conversations to lead to full-blown affairs. Take Beth and Bob, whom I mentioned earlier, for example. Both wandered into Christian chat rooms not knowing that the emotional connections made there could lead to adultery. Or take Julie, whose on-line affair led to a divorce. "I really wasn't wanting affairs from these men on-line," she says. "I really just wanted someone that would talk to me ... and I could talk about everyday things and I thought they cared."

Not only did Julie have an unintended affair, she failed to find someone who could meet her deeper needs. "These people don't care," she says now. "They are just using each other. It truly is a meat market, and I don't think there are a lot of real feelings involved. Oh, in some crazy way they think there is, but there's also the fear that if you aren't on-line then they will find someone else. I guess that is why the people that are into that stay on-line so much. They are afraid of losing that partner— whoever they have been talking to. But it's inevitable, because no one can be on all the time, and sooner or later ... they find someone that is more interesting or seems to say all the right things all over again."[13]

Debbie, a thirty-six-year-old attorney from Los Angeles, wasn't looking for an affair; she just wanted someone to help her learn how to play a multiplayer game called Darkness Falls. One guy offered to help, but soon he started flirting with her. "I appreciated his help so much and wanted to continue getting it, so I innocently began flirting back," she said. "The flirtations grew, and soon enough we were having cybersex while we were in character. I grew less and less attracted to my husband, and the male character became my fantasy on-line husband in the game."

"I felt as though I had fallen in love with this character. My on-line husband and I began corresponding through email and expressed that love for each other and began talking on the phone. I started spending less time with my [real] husband and more time ... on-line. Pretty soon I was missing court appearances because I couldn't get off the game. Luckily for me, my on-line husband [dumped me] after a year and a half.... My God, it was the worst feeling in the world. I felt like I had lost everything in the world that mattered to me. I left the game because I hurt so much."[14]

Both Debbie and Julie experienced a pattern that occurs frequently in relationships and has carried over to the Internet: the sex/intimacy exchange. "Women often give sex to get intimacy," says psychologist Dr. James Dobson, "and men give intimacy to get sex."[15] Internet chat rooms, newsgroups, and even on-line games have a way of bringing those tendencies together.

At first, a man may seem truly interested in discussing a favorite author with a woman in a literary newsgroup. As their conversation grows in intimacy, however, he may begin to pry about erotic interests. The woman who has invested in that relationship and has allowed it to meet a need for her may decide to respond in kind. "Having a meaningful relationship seems impossible for me," says the woman who is looking for a knight in shining armor. "I start to get attached emotionally and it scares men off; they just want free sex."[16]

A clandestine Internet relationship can seem fun for a season—swapping faceless messages can create the exhilaration of a masquerade ball. It's tempting to stay in an environment where your strengths can outweigh your weaknesses. Yet after that season is over, what most people want is someone who will love them for who they really are. Especially when they're not at their best—when they're throwing up, when they have morning breath, or when they've just tripped up a flight of stairs. They desire the kind of intimacy where they are known for who they are—warts and all—and are still loved.[17]

Regrettably, that realization may not come until after they have developed a cybersex addiction or damaged their marriage with an on-line affair. What is your situation? Do you anxiously look forward to your next opportunity to connect with someone on-line? Do you prefer your on-line persona to who you are in real life? Have you developed an emotional relationship with someone on-line behind your spouse's back?

If you have had an adulterous on-line affair or show signs of cybersex addiction, you really need the help of a professional counselor. Few people are able to work their way back toward healthy sexuality and intimacy without the help of a professional who can guide them through unresolved emotional conflicts.

Chapter Six

Porn

Brad's heart raced as he turned on his computer and went on-line. Maybe he wouldn't go there tonight. Maybe he would be strong. Or maybe he just couldn't help himself. "Just a quick look," he thought as he typed in an address. His heart pumped even faster as the page downloaded and images of naked women started filling the screen. He absorbed it all and then moved on to another site and then another. He had seen plenty of pornographic images, but he had to keep looking, he had to get the high again.

This was the same high he had been chasing since he was eight years old. That's when porn had entered Brad's life. "At that age, I hadn't heard of the 'birds and the bees,' so there was no way for me to know what the people in the pictures were doing," Brad remembers. "However, with viewing those pictures there also came an urge—I knew that what I was see-ing was dirty, and that made it all the more exciting. I remem-ber my pulse quickening and the adrenaline rushing through my body. I had my first 'hit' of porn, and I was hooked."[1]

Over the next few years Brad viewed pornographic maga-zines occasionally and sometimes stayed up late trying to see what he could on cable television.

In high school, Brad worked hard to hide a porn habit behind his clean-cut image as a star baseball player and youth group leader. "I went into college with a feeling that I would never beat my porn habit—that it would always be there." At college, Brad discovered Internet porn, sneaking peeks in the school computer lab on several occasions.

His on-line porn habit really took hold when he went home during the summer after his sophomore year. "I convinced my parents to hook up to this cool thing called the 'Internet.' They didn't know that the Internet would give me unlimited access to thousands and thousands of pornographic pictures. I remember thinking, 'this is going to be fun.' I would start around eleven at night and go until four or five in the morning—thinking I had only been on-line an hour." This pattern occurred nearly every Friday and Saturday and a couple of times during the week.

So here he was again, chasing after the high late into the night. As 5 A.M. rolled around, Brad started bargaining with God the way he had so many times in the past—promising not to do it again. This time he added in desperation, "Please help me, I don't know what to do."

Cybersex Addiction

Brad was addicted. He just couldn't get off the porn roller coaster. He knew the highs and lows well by now—the building sexual tension and climax followed by embarrassment, guilt, and new resolutions not to do it again ... until the next time.

Yet as so many men (and even some women) have discovered, each time it gets harder to resist. A recent article in *Men's Health* magazine described the Pavlovian conditioning that Internet sex can cause for the typical man:

"Now he can't look at a bland, beige computer without feeling a sexual charge. It starts in his groin and flows up his spine until his brain is dizzy with expectation." The writer goes on to explain that many on-line porn surfers never had a problem before they went on-line. "They certainly never felt like prisoners of a sexual compulsion," he writes, "until now. For some, curiosity has progressed to obsession. They don't mean to like electronic sex so much, but they do. And the need grows. They require more and more to keep from getting bored."[2]

An estimated 8 percent of men and 3 percent of women in the United States struggle with an addiction to on-line sexual experiences. This estimate comes from recent applications of Dr. Patrick Carnes' breakthrough research on sexual addiction.[3]

Building on the research of Carnes and others, Dr. Al Cooper, of the San Jose Marital and Sexuality Centre, identified five traits that distinguish cyber sexual compulsion. The first trait is denial, in which the user frequently minimizes, seeks to justify, or lies about his or her hidden activities. The second trait involves unsuccessful repeated efforts to stop the activity—continual resolutions that are repeatedly broken. Another trait is an inordinate amount of time spent on the activity—fantasizing, planning opportunities to indulge, and then spending time hiding the activity. A trait that may grow from subtle to more obvious is a negative impact on work, hobbies, and time with friends and family. Finally, a common trait of cybersex addiction is a repetition of the behavior despite adverse consequences.[4]

Problem Among Christians

"For many years I had the belief that I was the only person who struggled with this sort of thing," Brad said. Clearly, however, Internet pornography use is a widespread problem. Every week, at least 10 percent of Americans (25 million people) visit cybersex sites, and sexual visits account for up to 60 percent of all Web site traffic.[5]

Last spring, I asked the polling firm Zogby International to conduct a survey for Focus on the Family regarding Internet sex. Twenty percent of the respondents said they had visited sexually oriented Web sites—a fairly high number, considering that individuals usually underreport sexual information. The number of sex site viewers was almost identical for the subset that described themselves as "born-again Christians."[6]

As a former pastor and the current manager of a care line for pastors at Focus on the Family, Eldon Fry recognizes the extent of porn struggles among Christians. "One out of five of the calls on our pastoral care line has to do with sexual misconduct. The majority of those calls have to do with pornography, and the majority of the pornography calls are tied to the Internet."[7]

Tragically, hidden Internet habits are pushing a growing number of Christian leaders into legal trouble. Last fall, a judge sentenced Lawrence Kilbourn, founding pastor of a Methodist church in Bradenton, Florida, to seven years in prison after FBI agents found 3,700 child porn photos on his computer.[8] The month before that, a San Francisco area priest pled guilty to five felony counts of attempting to distribute harmful material to a minor over the Internet.[9]

For these men, and thousands of other Christians, Internet sex has proven to be a virtual prostitute just as seductive and dangerous as the prostitutes Solomon warned of in Proverbs: "For the lips of an adulteress drip honey, and her speech is smoother than oil; but in the end she is bitter as gall, sharp as a double-edged sword. Her feet go down to death; her steps lead straight to the grave" (Prv 5:3-5).

Problem Among Women

"Most of my life I have been stimulated most by touching," the woman told Dr. Schneider. "It was strange how pictures could stimulate a woman as much as it did me. I stumbled across a porn site by typing in a business address wrong. I went back out of curiosity. Within a matter of days I was doing it on a daily basis; within a matter of weeks, that is all I did. It literally took control and consumed my life. I went from joining all the free stuff, to anything I could to feed my addiction. I began to lie to my husband about working overtime just so I could continue to feed it. I didn't want to go home. I lost my mind in such a short time that I could not function at work or at home. The pictures I placed before me would haunt me day and night. I became very withdrawn and depressed."

This woman, thirty-five and married, represents a growing percentage of women who now struggle with pornography— a problem frequently perceived to be limited to men. Schneider found that many of the women in her survey of self-identified cybersex participants tended to follow an established pattern of focusing on relational aspects of sex. However, several were "visually oriented consumers of pornography"—objectifying men and indicating that they were looking for sex, not a relationship. "These women," Schneider points out, "identify more with traditional male sexual addiction stereotypes."[10]

"Younger women are more likely to find themselves compulsively drawn to pornography," explains Marnie Ferree, a counselor specializing in female sex addiction issues. "Sometimes they are conditioned by early abuse or are pulled in by men who share it with them, but many are just drawn in after growing up in a visually saturated culture."[11]

Supply and Demand

The word "pornography" comes from the Greek word *pornographos*, which literally means "writing about prostitutes." Despite debates about its legal and cultural definition, pornography is generally understood to be any material that depicts erotic behavior and is designed to cause sexual excitement.

For centuries, men (and some women) have looked to various forms of pornography as a counterfeit means to satisfy a natural sexual desire and curiosity. The supply of pornography, however, has not always been as rampant as it is today. In fact, it was seen as a vice of the wealthy in Tiberius Caesar's era. When he wanted to see erotic images, Tiberius had to import special hand-drawn scrolls from Egypt, or invite young men and women trained in sexual practices to perform in his palace.[12]

Since that time, the printing press, modern film technology, and VCRs have substantially increased the number of pornographic images available to the general public. The sexual revolution and the relaxed legal guidelines of the past thirty years have further increased the supply of and demand for pornography in America. Now, the Internet has sparked a sexual revolution of its own—housing a staggering collection of all stripes of pornographic images, available in the most efficient, anonymous, and cost-effective format ever.

This fundamental sea change in the supply of pornography has inevitably increased demand. "We're seeing a whole population of clients who have never had a history with [a pornography] problem," says Dr. Robert Weiss, clinical director of the Sexual Recovery Institute in Los Angeles. "But for the first time, they're beginning one activity and getting hooked."[13] Dr. Al Cooper estimates that at least 17 percent of current cybersex addicts didn't have a problem with porn before they went on-line but became compulsively drawn to sex sites.[14]

The Internet, it appears, facilitates and accelerates compulsive use of pornography. As I mentioned in the last chapter, Dr. Kimberly Young has found that the combination of anonymity, convenience, and escape can create an environment on-line that makes compulsive behavior more likely.

Anonymity

When Brad first saw a guy in his college computer lab looking at a *Playboy* site he remembers thinking, "Oh, wow, you can get that stuff on-line?" Before then he had endured the embarrassment of going to a store, where he could be seen buying a magazine or renting a video.

Dr. Jennifer Schneider points out that Christians often fall into a category of cybersex users identified as "at risk"—"persons who had no prior history of sexual compulsivity, yet when faced with the anonymity, accessibility, and affordability of the computer, found themselves spending substantial time and energy on cybersex activities."[15]

Eldon Fry has spoken with several Christian leaders who follow that pattern. "These guys share with me that they had suppressed their temptation for pornography after leaving seminary because they didn't want to be seen looking for porn in public. Now all the barriers are down, and behind closed doors, during long hours at the office, they crumble."[16]

The promise of anonymity tempts on-line surfers into thinking that they can indulge sexual fantasies without hurting their carefully maintained reputations at home, the office, or church.

Convenience

Not only did the Internet save Brad the embarrassment of being seen paying for a pornographic magazine or video at a store, it saved him the trouble of having to leave the house to begin with. Driven by a highly efficient global distribution system, the Internet pipes directly into the house more content than any one pornographic store could keep in stock. It also provides service around the clock and at any location where an Internet connection is available.

Convenient access to a large volume of pornography proved to be a great temptation for Brad. "With the unlimited number of sites out there, and tons of free stuff, there's always the prospect of something better. The search for more consumes your time."

"That's what makes sex on-line far more compelling than any shrink-wrapped smut," writes the author of the *Men's Health* article on cybersex. "It's instant gratification in endless variety—you never get to the end of the magazine and have to start looking at the same pictures again. With old porn, once you view it, you've consumed it. You've chewed the flavor out of the gum. This can't be done on the Net. The gum never runs out of flavor."[17]

The convenience of on-line pornography, however, also makes it much easier for someone craving strong stimulation to accelerate beyond *Playboy*-quality porn and into the realm of hardcore and often illegal stuff like bestiality, bondage, and child porn. Whereas such material isn't even available on the shelves at local porn shops, it's only a hyperlink away from normal sexual content on-line.

"In the last couple of years, the more porn I've viewed, the less sensitive I am to certain porn that I used to find offensive," one man told Dr. Schneider. "Now I get turned on by some of it. The sheer quantity of porn on the Net has done this. It's so easy to click on certain things out of curiosity in the privacy of your home, and the more you see them, the less sensitized you are. I used to only be into the soft-core porn showing the beauty of the female form. Now I'm into explicit hardcore."[18]

Finally, the Internet makes it more convenient for people with shared sexual interests to form communities of support and justification for their fetishes. "Part of the problem with cybersex is, it reinforces and normalizes sexual disorders," says Dr. Robert Weiss. "A man may have had a passing interest in teenaged girls, but he'd never go into a bookstore and try to buy child pornography. Sitting in his living room, he finds tons of teen sites and thinks maybe it's not such a big problem."[19] Through various Web sites, newsgroups, bulletin boards, and chat rooms, people with perverse sexual fantasies can easily and anonymously assemble. The group support they provide often breaks down any remaining inhibitions participants may have had about these fantasies.

Escape

"Many times I would run to pornography because I just wanted to feel good," Brad remembers. "Maybe I was having a bad day; maybe my self-esteem was low; or I was stressed out. Pornography provided the outlet for me to be able to forget about those things for awhile and actually feel good about myself." Brad also ran to porn when relationships proved too difficult. "I was very much withdrawn. I was shy. Relationships seemed very difficult to maintain. I didn't feel like putting forth the effort, because I wasn't good at it and a lot had failed earlier. Whenever a relationship did fail, porn was always there to run to. There was no interaction required and no judgment."

That's the pattern Gene McConnell sees as he travels around the country talking about how shame drove his own porn use. "It seems to meet a need for intimacy in the person who can't be vulnerable in relationships—who doesn't want to show his real self," he says.[20]

Pornography, in itself, it seems, offers an escape from the pressures of life and from the headaches often associated with meaningful relationships. The Internet increases that sense of escape, providing more convenient and extensive outlets for fantasies. The Internet also enhances the high that comes with such an escape. "It works ... quickly and it's ... instantly intense," says Dr. Robert Weiss, who describes cybersex as the "crack cocaine of sexual addiction."[21]

By providing a combination of sexual enjoyment and escape from negative emotions, on-line pornography can pull users into a downward spiral. Dr. Al Cooper explains the process in a journal article on Internet sexual compulsivity:

Reinforcement occurs both from the sexual enjoyment as well as the distraction from more uncomfortable emotional stress. For example, if a person feels anxious or depressed and experiences relief from these feelings through the online behavior, then the latter is reinforced. Thus, an individual can develop a cycle of behavior where a negative emotion is experienced, Internet use ensues, sexual behavior occurs, and negative emotion is temporarily blocked, thus reinforcing the cycle. With each additional enactment of the cycle, feelings of shame, decreased self-esteem, and loss of control increase, which in turn, fuels a downward spiral.[22]

Subtle Dangers to Intimate Relationships

The Internet environment can push casual viewers of pornography over the edge and into a cybersex addiction, a serious problem that needs to be recognized and addressed. However, casual porn viewers should recognize that potential addiction is not the only problem they are flirting with. A private habit of going to sexual pictures for fulfillment brings other understated dangers.

In his book *The Centerfold Syndrome*, Dr. Gary R. Brooks identifies five subtle problems that develop in men after viewing even the mildest pornography: The first is voyeurism—an obsession with looking at women rather than interacting with them. Second is objectification—women become objects rated by size, shape and harmony of body parts. Next is validation—men who don't achieve their dream women are left feeling cheated or unmanly. Similar to validation is trophyism—the idea that beautiful women are collectibles who show the world who a man is. Most importantly, pornography develops in men a fear of true intimacy—an inability to relate to women in an honest and intimate way despite deep loneliness.[23]

Brooks explains that porn erodes intimacy because it "pays scant attention to men's needs for sensuality and intimacy while exalting their sexual needs."[24] In other words, porn ruins men's appetites—their healthy sexual hunger for their wives (or future wives). C.S. Lewis once wrote, "You must not isolate the sexual pleasure and try to get it by itself, anymore than you ought to try to get the pleasures of taste without swallowing and digesting, by chewing things and spitting them out again."[25] By offering arousal without intimacy, pornography feeds men's sexual cravings with the equivalent of sticky sweets loaded with empty calories.

"[Pornography] thwarted my development of appropriate relational and coping skills," Jody Burgin told the congressional panel. "I feel it caused me to objectify women, seeing them as nothing more than a means to satisfy my desires. I grew less satisfied with my wife's affection, physical appearance, sexual curiosity, and sexual performance.... Sex without emotional involvement became increasingly important. It created feelings of power and control and led me to becoming a manipulative and controlling person to those closest to me."[26]

As I mentioned in the last chapter on cyber relationships, in a fallen world, everyone brings imperfections into their relationships. Even the best marriages face doubts, fears, and hurt. Dr. Schaumburg explains that men and women can find real intimacy in loving, committed marriages with open communication. The temptation everyone faces, however, is the desire to take a shortcut—to settle for what Schaumburg calls "false intimacy."[27] Instead of going through the effort required for real intimacy, people often settle for an illusion— an airbrushed image, a virtual reality, a cyberaffair—something that seems to give a high without hurt, ecstasy without expectations, fulfillment without faults.

This was what happened to "Jeff," an addiction counselor who lost his job as a pastor due to sexual sin. "I desired so desperately to be loved and accepted," he says, "but I settled for the quick fix. With pornography, there was no fear of rejection, no possibility for disappointment. In that fantasy world, I was always loved, desired, and accepted—it seemed easier than taking the risks involved in pursuing loving relationships in the real world."[28]

And don't think your spouse doesn't notice when your appetite changes. When Dr. Schneider surveyed spouses of compulsive porn surfers, she found that all of them felt hurt, betrayed, or rejected. "All of these women felt unfavorably compared," she says. "Sixty-eight percent reported that their partner had become disinterested in sex with them. Twenty-two percent attributed their divorce from these partners to the Internet."

Unsafe at Any Speed

Has a stolen glance steamrolled into an uncontrollable habit for you? Are your emotions trapped in a roller coaster of anxiety, fantasy, and guilt? Are walls of shame and denial going up between you and your friends or family? Has a taste of false intimacy spoiled your appetite for meaningful intimacy with your spouse?

God directs us to abstain from sexual immorality (see Acts 15:29). Christians may be able to participate in on-line games or auctions in moderation, but moderation is simply not an option when it comes to surfing for porn. Consumer advocacy guru Ralph Nader complained that the 1961 Chevy Corvair was "Unsafe at Any Speed," pointing to the fact that the sporty vehicle would flip over going 35 mph on a dry road.[29] Similarly, the threat of addiction for many porn surfers and the reality of subtle dangers for everyone else make on-line pornography unsafe at any level.

Chapter Seven

Overcoming an Internet Addiction

There is no simple formula for overcoming abusive or addictive Internet use. There are, however, consistent elements of treatment that overlap when you take into account therapy for traditional addiction, emerging theories for Internet addiction treatment, testimonials of recent Internet addicts, and biblical principles shared by pastors and Christian counselors.

Elements of Success

Reviewing these areas, I found at least five elements that are essential for overcoming an Internet addiction and maintaining long-term sobriety:

1.) *A Candid and Accurate Assessment of Your Problem Followed by a Willingness to Change*

Before you can treat any problem, you have to know what it is and accept that it is actually something you are willing to address. Many addicts have to hit bottom before they finally admit their problem and commit to recovery. It doesn't have to be that way. It's best to get help before you get caught or get in trouble. More details, and resources to help you understand your specific area of struggle, are available at the end of this chapter.

2.) A Community of Support

Addiction is an isolating experience. You need friends, family, and people who understand your struggle to help you break out of addictive behavior. The following chapter provides an overview of the various components of a support community— friends and family, a Christian counselor, a support group, and accountability partners.

3.) Immediate and Ongoing Action to Change Harmful Behavior

Breaking free from out-of-control behavior depends on the actions you take today to "stop the bleeding" and the actions you take tomorrow to create a healthy environment for future on-line use. These steps are discussed in chapter 9.

4.) Understanding and Addressing Underlying Thoughts and Emotions

Behavior modification is not sufficient in and of itself. If you don't take the time to address the thoughts and emotions that drive your addictive behavior, you may easily relapse or move on to another addiction. More on this topic can be found in chapter 10.

5.) A Restored Relationship With God

God sees you in your struggle and offers unconditional love and forgiveness, but how do you see God? What do you know about him? Do you know how to receive his forgiveness? Can you trust him to guide your recovery? Chapter 11 talks about the imperative of a restored relationship with God.

How each of these elements is specifically applied will depend upon your circumstances. The emphasis and timing may be affected by outside conditions such as job loss, marital breakup, or legal trouble. The approach will also be different based on the type of addiction you are facing—a general Internet compulsion, a gambling addiction, a cybersex addiction, or something else. You may be able to make some progress on your own in the areas of behavior and thought modification but you will likely need the encouragement and wisdom of your support community to work through the other elements. A licensed Christian counselor can help you develop a comprehensive treatment plan that includes all of these elements.

Tackling Your Problem

After honestly reviewing your on-line habits, do you recognize a negative impact on your time, your work, your relationships, or your health and reputation? If you do, then your Internet use, whether addictive or not, requires attention. The first question to ask yourself at this point is "Do you really want to overcome your addiction? Do you want to go beyond just doing damage control?"

For any problem to be addressed, there has to be a breaking point. Ideally, someone who is struggling with abusive Internet behavior will reflect on his or her actions and recognize a problem. Yet addictive behavior usually involves denial and desensitization. A breaking point often has to come in the form of confrontation (frequently by a spouse), getting caught, getting fired from work, or even experiencing consequences for breaking the law.

"Most people only get help after they get caught," says counselor Dr. Harry Schaumburg.[1] Yet getting caught, he insists, can be a good thing, because it connects a person's private and public worlds and forces the issue to be addressed. "I wished I had gotten caught tons of times, but it never happened," says Brad, referring to his pornography struggle. "Obviously, at the time, I was covering my tracks; but deep down, I wanted help so bad that I wanted to get caught."

Getting caught was the pivotal point for Stewart, a man who contacted me through the Pure Intimacy Web site. "My wife, who thought I had kicked the habit, so to speak, found out everything and blew up," he said. "Something clicked this time, however. It finally clicked that I was a bona fide pornography addict and that my addiction was just as real and dangerous as crack cocaine."

Many remain in denial. "People often don't want to dive into the ugliness of their sin and the effect on their relationships," says Dr. Steve Fetrow. He recalls a client asking him, "What's the recovery time for someone who just wants to dabble in on-line porn for about thirty minutes a week?" Fetrow responded, "forever," but the man didn't understand his response. "Because you are morally superior," he explained, "you haven't addressed the issues, you think you're just dabbling, you don't want help, you don't want to wrestle with the sin, and if that's where you're at, you'll be there forever."[2]

Unless they reach a breaking point, however, people rarely focus on their fallen nature. In other words, they allow their problem to take them to the bottom before they start looking up.

When you are finally ready to admit that your behavior is out of control and that you need help, the best place to start is to ask a Christian addictions counselor for a professional diagnosis—a closer examination of your struggle to access appropriate treatment. If you are not aware of a qualified counselor in your area, you can contact the counseling department at the nonprofit ministry Focus on the Family for a referral. (Call 719-531-3400 weekdays between 9:00 A.M. and 4:30 P.M. Mountain Time and ask for the counseling department.)

Resources for Understanding Your Problem

General On-Line Surfing, Auctions, and Games
Web Sites
- Center for Online Addiction/Dr. Kimberly Young (www.netaddiction.com)
- The Center for Internet Studies/Dr. David Greenfield (www.virtual-addiction.com)
- Computer Addiction Services/Maressa Hecht Orzack, Ph.D. (www.computeraddiction.com)

Books
- *Caught in the Net* by Dr. Kimberly Young (New York: John Wiley & Son, Inc., 1998)
- *Virtual Addiction: Help for Netheads, Cyberfreaks, and Those Who Love Them* by David D. Greenfield (Oakland, Calif.: New Harbinger Productions, 1999)

Gambling and Day-Trading
Web Sites
- Center for Online Addiction on Gambling (www.netaddiction.com/net_compulsions.htm)
- Center for Online Addiction on Daytrading (www.netaddiction.com/daytrading.htm)
- Arnie & Sheila Wexler Associates—resource on com pulsive gambling (www.aswexler.com)
- Compulsive Gambling Center/ Dr. Valerie C. Lorenz (www.lostbet.com)
- Special feature on gambling by Focus on the Family (www.family.org/gambling)

Books
- *Gambling Addiction: The Problem, the Pain, and the Pathway to Recovery* by John M. Eades (1999)

- *Bad Bet: The Inside Story of the Glamour, Glitz, and Danger of America's Gambling Industry* by Timothy L. O'Brien (New York: Times Books, 1998)
- *The Luck Business: The Devastating Consequences and Broken Promises of America's Gambling Explosion* by Robert Goodman (New York: Free Press, 1996)
- *Pathological Gambling: The Making of a Medical Problem* by Brian Castellani (New York: University of New York Press, 2000)

On-Line Pornography and Affairs

Web Sites Addressing Sex Addiction

- Christians for Sexual Integrity (www.SexualIntegrity.org)
- Healing for Women/Marnie C. Ferree, M.A. (www.healingforwomen.org)
- Center for Online Addiction on Cybersex Addiction (www.netaddiction.com/cybersexual_addiction.htm)
Web Sites Addressing Pornography and Other Sex Problems
- Pure Intimacy (www.pureintimacy.org)
- Web site of Dr. Cliff and Joyce Penner (www.PassionateCommitment.com)
- National Coalition for the Protection of Children and Families (www.nationalcoalition.org)

Books on Sexual Problems

- *False Intimacy* by Dr. Harry Schaumburg (Colorado Springs: NavPress, 1997)
- *Women, Sex and Addiction* by Charlotte Davis Kasl (New York: HarperCollins, 1990)
- *Cybersex Exposed: Recognizing the Obsession* by Jennifer P. Schneider and Robert L. Weiss (Minneapolis: Hazelden Publishing and Education, 2001)

- *Out of the Shadows: Understanding Sexual Addiction* by Patrick Carnes (Center City, Minn.: Hazelden Information Education, 1992)
- *Don't Call it Love: Recovery from Sex Addiction* by Patrick Carnes (New York: Bantam Books, 1992)

Books on Pornography

- *The Centerfold Syndrome: How Men Can Overcome Objectification and Achieve Intimacy with Women* by Dr. Gary Brooks (San Francisco: Jossey-Bass, 1995)
- *Every Man's Battle: Winning the War on Sexual Temptation One Victory at a Time* by Stephen Arterburn and Fred Stoeker with Mike Yorkey (Colorado Springs: WaterBrook Press, 2000)
- *Men's Secret Wars* by Patrick Means (Grand Rapids, Mich.: Revell, 1996)
- *The Final Freedom: Pioneering Sexual Addiction Recovery* by Doug Weiss (Fort Worth, Tex.: Discovery Press, 1998)
- *Faithful and True* by Mark Laaser (Grand Rapids, Mich.: Zondervan, 1996)
- *The Skinner Box Effect: Sexual Addiction and Online Pornography* by T.M. Grundner, Ed.D. (New York: Writer's Club Press, 2000)
- *The Silent War: Ministering to Those Trapped in the Deception of Pornography* by Henry J. Rogers (Los Angeles: New Leaf Press, 2000).

Chapter Eight

A Community of Support

Recovery from abusive or addictive Internet behavior, especially cybersex, depends on real and restored relationships. Secret indulgent behavior can drive a wedge between you and your friends and family. You need the encouragement and accountability of those relationships. If your habit has grown into an addiction, then you also need the support of people who understand your problem—support groups, Christian counselors, and accountability partners. Along with friends and family, these form the community of support that is vital to recovery.

Reconnecting With Friends and Family

"Relationship problems are often the core issue behind Internet addiction," says Dr. Steve Fetrow, "and recovery involves learning to love well within your relationships."[1] Learning to love well, however, is not an easy task, because relationships are complicated and require effort to build and maintain.

It's the disappointments and unpredictability of relationships, after all, that often lead people to addictive Internet habits to begin with. The person who can't seem to make friends or impress people around him escapes into an on-line game where he can win the respect of other players and enjoy a form of companionship. The wife who can't seem to work out communication issues with her husband finds someone on-line who says all the things she wants to hear. The single guy who feels awkward around women finds it much safer to interact with anonymous pictures of women on-line.

The Internet hurts relationships by offering a place to escape from the complications of real-life relationships and by meeting a relational need with pseudorelational experiences. Recovery necessitates returning to real relationships.

If you are single and don't have vital relationships, then you should. You need to reinvest in your relationships with your family, coworkers, classmates, people in your church, and others. That's what Brad discovered in his struggle with pornography. "I'm relational at my core—like everyone else," Brad realizes now. "Despite how difficult it is to have relationships— I need that and I have to push myself to be in relationship with others." Brad says he recognizes now how much relationships can replace the void that pornography used to fill.

If you are in a committed relationship, you need to seek forgiveness for lost time and attention and any other consequences of your on-line behavior. Most importantly, however, you need to start addressing any relational problems from which the Internet helped you to escape. That's especially true if you have given in to the lure of on-line pornography or affairs, activities that are frequently fueled by larger relationship problems.

In her review of numerous cases of cybersex addiction, Dr. Young identified six common preexisting relationship problems: "1) poor communication skills, 2) unresolved sexual dissatisfaction, 3) differences in child-rearing practices, 4) a recent relocation from support of family and friends, 5) financial problems, and 6) poor conflict resolution skills."[2] Cybersex and other on-line addictions may alleviate the pressure of these kinds of problems but they cannot solve them.

If you are finding these problems insurmountable, you and your spouse will very likely need the help of a trusted marriage counselor. In conjunction with the counselor, you will probably also need the safe and focused environment of a support group to work through the struggle of compulsive sexual desires.

Confession

All of these steps for relationship recovery assume that your problem is out in the open. If no one knows about your problem, then you've got to tell someone. "The devil uses secrets to keep you in bondage, and once you reveal your secret, it is like the key that unlocks the chains of bondage," a man named J.B. told me in an email.[3]

Sharing your problem with someone else at least doubles your ability to recover. You've probably noticed how ineffective your attempts to fix your secret little problem have been. What you are missing is the power that comes from confessing to another person—from tearing down the wall between your public and private worlds.

Confession is all the more important—and difficult—in a marriage. Secret habits and lies about on-line activity can suck the oxygen out of relationships by damaging trust and transparency. Confession clears the air. Unfortunately, confessions are rarely initiated. "Disclosure usually happens spontaneously— you get caught," says Dr. Schneider. "The minority, however, have the opportunity to initiate and that's the better option."[4]

Although confession is ultimately good for the relationship, it will inevitably involve discomfort. You can't be sure how your spouse will respond. Even if he or she is relieved that you have confessed, your spouse will likely feel hurt or betrayed. You will have to work to regain his or her trust. For that reason, you have to mean it. You have to be prepared to not only confess a problem but truly repent, to take concrete steps away from your harmful behavior.

Women, especially, have to be careful about confessing a sexual problem, because men often know less about how to deal with it. According to Dr. Schneider, their shame is great; men often get angry, and can be very controlling. A woman who is ready to confess sexual sin needs a safe place, such as the office of a pastor or counselor, in which to do it.

Professional Counseling

Brad wrote a suicide note, hopped in his car, and just started driving. "I knew I had a problem and I wanted to get out," he remembers. "I tried to stop viewing Internet pornography but I gave up—I thought this was a problem I would always live with."

A few days earlier, Brad had confessed his struggle to his parents but they didn't know what to do with it and he didn't think things were getting better. "I felt like I wasn't being heard. It was like a volcano exploding. I needed someone to talk to and to help me work through everything."

Fortunately, Brad drove to Dallas instead of driving off a cliff somewhere. In Dallas, he checked into the New Life clinic, where his parents eventually joined him for counseling. There, Brad found professionals who were equipped to handle his confession and guide him and his parents through underlying issues that were driving his problem.

Between individual sessions with a counselor and group therapy, Brad started opening up. "I had never been in anything like that—I was spilling everything that had happened."

Brad says that it was valuable for him to share with people who knew how to take it. "It helped me see the lies I had believed—that [I was] the only one and that if people knew, they wouldn't want to talk to me. But in this group, I shared that side of me and people were very encouraging."

Brad's individual counselor helped moderate a family discussion. Through that process, Brad learned about his dad's struggle with pornography. "That helped me to understand why I was susceptible and why our relationship had been like it was."

When You Need Professional Help

Brad's problem was out of control. He couldn't fix it with simple behavior modification efforts. He needed professional diagnosis and treatment in order to work through deeply rooted emotional and spiritual issues that lay beneath the surface. Perhaps that's where you are—unable to abstain from addictive Internet behavior. Like the struggle the apostle Paul described, you may constantly find yourself doing things that you don't want to do and unable to do the things you want to do.

Maybe you have been underestimating the effect that childhood trauma—sexual abuse, loss of a parent, or an alcoholic parent—has had on you. Maybe you have been unable to understand the connection between your behavior and a breakdown in intimacy and communication with your spouse. Or maybe you've recently bottomed out—gotten caught, lost your job, or been arrested—and you need some serious help to start finding your way back to normal.

If you see yourself in one of these scenarios, you need to find a professional counselor or treatment center whose work is built on a relationship with Jesus Christ.

"There are several things you can do on your own to reorient the thoughts and behavior associated with your problem," says Christian counselor Rob Jackson, "but counseling is key for processing unresolved emotional conflicts that lie beneath the surface."[5] He recommends that addicts initiate counseling from the start.

How About Pastoral Counseling?

Your pastor and other leaders in your church can be an integral part of your recovery, but you should be aware that church leaders perform some roles better than others. Several men who contacted me through the Pure Intimacy Web site expressed disappointment with how little their pastors seemed to understand Internet addictions. At least one pastor told an addict to just get rid of his computer and that would fix the problem. "There's an education gap out there," says Rob Jackson, who travels frequently to churches to do workshops on sexual addiction. "Often pastors try to help, but their advice ends up being shaming, legalizing, or minimizing."[6]

Rob recommends that pastors concentrate on their area of strength, serving as shepherds and spiritual advisors. In their role as shepherds, pastors can be advocates for members of their "flock" who need direction in recovery. Rob encourages pastors and other church leaders to be an adjunct to a recovery team, which may include a professional counselor, a support group or accountability group, and the friends and family of the addict. The church leader serves as the gatekeeper of resources, to determine spiritual appropriateness or safety and then to hold the team accountable to the therapeutic process.

Furthermore, Rob believes the pastor or church leader

serves a valuable role in helping the addict work through unresolved spiritual conflicts. He insists that an addict's confusion about the nature of God's love and forgiveness is often what makes behavior modification alone ineffective.

What Is Intensive Counseling?

Typically, Christian counselors can schedule only an hour or two a week to see clients in their office. That kind of schedule is sufficient for a lot of the issues they handle, but it may drag recovery out. In his personal practice, Rob Jackson recommends that couples dealing with sex addiction consider accelerating their treatment. "I tell them that if they have sex addiction in a troubled marriage they will need to do a minimum of twenty one-hour sessions. Then I ask them if they would be willing to fly out and do that in a five-day period with follow-up by a local therapist, pastor, and support group instead."[7]

Intensive counseling can be especially helpful in a time of crisis—after contracting a sexually transmitted disease, ruining finances, getting fired, or having a marriage break up, for example. Willy Wooten, head of the Focus on the Family counseling department, tells me that the Chinese character for the word "crisis" is a combination of the characters for the words "disaster" and "opportunity." He encourages addicts to recognize that a crisis brings them to a fork in the road—either they can refuse to address their problems and progress toward disaster or they can see the crisis as an opportunity to seek recovery.[8] Regardless of the crisis, the intensive setting offers a place of retreat and focus where the addict can be serious about getting help. That sense of retreat is important because it temporarily eliminates distractions—work, TV, phones, kids, and especially the Internet—so that the addict can focus tightly on recovery.

Stone Gate Ministries, started by Dr. Harry Schaumburg, provides that kind of retreat experience. To get there, you drive away from the city lights and suburbs of Colorado Springs, Colorado, and through a dense wooded area called the Black Forest just north of the city. After a few miles the trees thin and you see a broad prairie open around you, with views for several miles. As the road turns to gravel, you wrap around and up onto a large mesa jutting out of the landscape. That's where Stone Gate sits, surrounded by mule deer, coyote, and foxes and staring at a view of Colorado's front range, including the majestic Pikes Peak.

Dr. Schaumburg says he did traditional brief counseling sessions for years and noticed that a lot of his clients were dropping out. "I think it's because a lot of them found themselves moving one step forward and two steps back," he says. "They would come in for an intense meeting where they concentrated on their problem for an hour and then they would go back to the distractions of everyday life. A week-to-week approach seems to be too little, too slow."[9]

Finding the Right Counselor or Program for You

A couple of ministries provide referral services that will help you find Christians who are qualified to address your specific area of need:

Focus on the Family counseling referral service
Call (719) 531-3400 on weekdays from 9:00 to 4:30. (MST) and ask for the counseling department.

Christians for Sexual Integrity (*CSI*)
(866) 224-6838 (toll free)
500 Lake Street, Suite 105
Excelsior, MN 55344
www.sexualintegrity.org

CSI's Call Center focuses on sexual problems. It is available between the hours of 9:00 A.M. and 5:00 P.M. (CST), Monday through Friday.

While these referral services specialize in making referrals for individual week-to-week counselors, they also can make some recommendations for intensive counseling and hospital programs. Here are some of the leading services that I recommend:

Intensive Counseling
Stone Gate Ministries
11509 Palmer Divide Road
Larkspur, CO 80118
Office@stonegateresources.org
www.stonegateresources.com
(303) 688-5680

Jackson Consulting
Rob Jackson, M.S., L.P.C., N.C.C.
(612) 207-7198
500 Lake Street, Suite 105
Excelsior, MN 55331
appointments@ChristianCounsel.com
www.christiancounsel.com

Christian Hospital Programs

New Life
1-800-NEW-LIFE
www.newlife.com

Rapha
1-800-383-HOPE
www.rapha-hope.com

Secular Hospital Programs

The Meadows
1655 N. Tegner St.
Wickenburg, AZ 85390
info@themeadows.org
www.themeadows.org
1-800-MEADOWS / Fax:(520) 684-3261

Illinois Institute for Addiction Recovery
at Proctor Hospital (includes new clinic for
computer/Internet addiction)
5409 North Knoxville
Peoria, IL 61614
(309) 691-1000
info@proctor.org
www.proctor.org/addict.html

Support Groups

When he was ten, Bill Wilson was abandoned by his alcoholic
father. Bill started drinking twelve years later and found himself

constantly reaching for a drink as a soldier and then as a businessman. Alcohol, he found, numbed depression and also helped him celebrate successes on Wall Street.

In 1935, Bill traveled to Akron, Ohio, on business. When his business deal collapsed, he started looking for a drink. Although he had tried to control his drinking habit several times before, he finally had a breakthrough. He figured that maybe he could fix his own problem by helping another alcoholic.

After a frenzied search for someone in the same boat, he located a man named Dr. Robert Smith. Dr. Smith felt skeptical about meeting, and promised Wilson only fifteen minutes of his time. Fifteen minutes turned into several hours and the Alcoholics Anonymous movement was born. The concept for the group grew around the idea that only an alcoholic can help another alcoholic.

Soon, Bill's in-laws' house back in New York became something of a meeting place for drunks. As various and sundry guests gathered for meetings, Bill would introduce himself: "My name is Bill W., and I'm an alcoholic."[10]

Bill Wilson and Dr. Smith are considered the grandfathers of the twelve-step program—a format in which people with shared problems meet together to recognize their need for a higher power and to systematically work toward recovery. People with problems other than alcohol have adapted the twelve steps to address everything from smoking to eating too much junk food.

The simple power of twelve-step programs is that they create a supportive environment in which addicts can safely confess a problem, release it to God for his intervention, and then work alongside an accountability group to restore relationships with those around them. By providing a methodical format for adequately recognizing and addressing a problem, twelve-step programs formalize a process that can otherwise get short-circuited when someone tries to recover on his own. To ensure that no one is trying to fix a problem on his own, twelve-step programs typically match participants with sponsors who serve as accountability partners.

Both Christian and secular addictions counselors recognize the benefit of including a twelve-step program in their clients' recovery efforts—especially in the areas of thought and behavior management. "I have never seen a female sex addict recover without being part of a group," says Marnie Ferree, a Christian counselor and lecturer. "The inclusion of a support group in a treatment approach is a given if the addict has an intimacy disorder or has experienced long-term or intense periods of acting out," says Rob Jackson.[11]

Currently, there are no national twelve-step programs for Internet addiction. There are, however, groups that specifically address sex addiction and gambling addiction, problems that are exacerbated (and sometimes initiated) by the Internet. The value of twelve-step groups is that the core principles and structure of the meetings can be easily adapted to other issues. For that reason, people with a variety of addictions often benefit from Alcoholics Anonymous, even if they don't specifically have an alcohol addiction.

Looking at the essence of the typical twelve-step program, you can see how generic the steps are:

Step 1: Admitting powerlessness over addiction.
Step 2: Recognizing God as a higher power.
Step 3: Turning lives and wills over to God's care.
Step 4: Taking a moral inventory of oneself.
Step 5: Admitting to God, to oneself, and to others the nature of wrongs committed.

Step 6: Becoming ready to have God remove character defects.

Step 7: Humbly asking God to remove shortcomings.

Step 8: Making a list of everyone harmed by addiction, and becoming willing to make amends to them all.

Step 9: Making direct amends to people harmed, wherever possible, except when doing so would injure them.

Step 10: Continuing to take a personal inventory and promptly admitting when wrong.

Step 11: Seeking through prayer and meditation to improve relationship with God, praying for knowledge of his will and the power to carry it out.

Step 12: Upon having a spiritual awakening, taking that message to other addicts and practicing the principles of the twelve steps in all of one's affairs.[12]

"Christians would do well to live by these steps," says addictions counselor Steve Earll. Steve makes that point because he realizes that Christians are often skeptical about the twelve-step approach. Often they are not aware of the biblical basis for groups like Alcoholics Anonymous. It is not widely known that the Bible and a couple of popular religious devotionals of the day were the main inspiration for the format of the twelve steps. In the rush to mainstream support groups, however, several chapters have secularized the twelve steps, and some are now even hostile to Christian participants.[13] Some groups, like Gamblers Anonymous, built their program on a secular basis from the beginning.

For these reasons, Willy Wooten, head of the counseling department at Focus on the Family, adds a disclaimer whenever he talks about the role of a support group. "Not all groups are alike. Many are not Christian based," he says. "They often fail to identify their 'higher power' as God, the Father, and that leaves the spiritual force as some kind of nebulous New Age entity.

When Paul went to Athens he proclaimed who the unknown God was."[14]

Fortunately, numerous twelve-step groups retain their spiritual identity. Many communities have Alcoholics Anonymous groups that specifically add the word Christian to their name so participants will know what to expect. Recently, several churches and ministries began adapting their own versions of AA so that Christians would have an easier time finding an appropriate group.

A few years ago, a guy named Tim looked for a Christian-based support group to help him tackle a drinking problem and found it in a group called Overcomer's Outreach. Started by Bob and Pauline Bartosch, Overcomer's Outreach serves as a bridge between the church and groups such as Alcoholics Anonymous. Participants among the seven hundred Overcomer's Outreach groups throughout the United States address a variety of problems, including gambling, alcohol, and sex addictions. The group also welcomes spouses who have been hurt by their partners' problems.

The thing Tim appreciates most about the group is the same factor that drove Bill Wilson—a community of empathy. "Friends, family members, a counselor, or a pastor can only empathize so much with an addict," Tim says. He values receiving help from someone who can understand the power of his temptations and his weakness in a moment of decision.

Tim also points out that support groups help addicts to rebuild relationships. Not only are addicts able to build new relationships in a group that accepts them despite their shame, but they are also able to systematically evaluate and address the damage they have caused in their relationships with friends and family, and especially with God.

It's not just the steps that make this possible; it's the safe and open environment that groups try to maintain. Such an environment cannot be underestimated. Some addicts simply don't know anyone with whom they could feel comfortable sharing their problem. Furthermore, many participants have never been in relationships where they could open up without interruption or judgment. By offering a neutral environment for open communication between the addict and the spouse, support groups can aid in the restoration of damaged marriages.

"Ideally, a good support group is, first, a place where recovering addicts will find true acceptance and a sense of what unconditional love is all about," the Christian Recovery Connection Web site explains. "It is a safe, nonjudgmental setting where they can express struggles, thoughts, ideas, and feelings without fear of rejection. Hearing the stories of others with similar difficulties and how they overcame them gives the struggling addict great encouragement to go on in a life of sobriety."[15]

Finding the Right Group for You

Willy Wooten encourages addicts to attend only Christian support groups. When one is not available, he recommends that the addict supplement his or her attendance at a secular group with involvement in Overcomer's Outreach or with ongoing meetings with a Christian counselor. Willy also recommends that addicts work on building meaningful relationships beyond their support groups or counselors. "It's not healthy for recovering addicts to just bond with their counselor or members of their support group and not grow in relationships with friends and family members."[16] That kind of bonding often leads addicts to trade their original addiction for addiction to the support group instead.

The Christian Recovery Connection not only provides its viewers with a biblical perspective of the twelve steps, it offers a searchable directory of local support groups: crc.iugm.org/support.html. They recommend that pastors or counselors review support groups before referring their counselees. Two other groups who serve as guides to Christian support groups are the National Association for Christian Recovery and Christians in Recovery.

National Association for Christian Recovery
P.O. Box 215
Brea, CA 92822-0215
www.christianrecovery.com/nacr.htm
Voice: (714) 529-6227 Fax: (714) 529-1120

Christians in Recovery
P.O. Box 4422
Tequesta, FL 33469
admin@christians-in-recovery.org
www.christians-in-recovery.org/db

Christian Recovery Connection
www.crc.iugm.org

General Internet Addictions
Until a national Internet Addicts Anonymous group is launched, Overcomer's Outreach is probably the best bet for addressing Internet addictions that do not involve sex or gambling:
Overcomer's Outreach
520 N. Brookhurst, Suite 121

Anaheim, CA 92801
www.overcomersoutreach.org
1-800-310-3001 or (714) 491-3000

Gambling

If you have a gambling problem, or even a day-trading problem, you can find some help through Gambling Anonymous. However, Dr. Valerie Lorenz, executive director of the Compulsive Gambling Center in Baltimore, warns addicts that Gamblers Anonymous does not have a spiritual component and that it tends to have serious dropout rates. If you join a local G.A. you should plan to attend an Overcomer's Outreach or similar Christian group as well. Lorenz points out that Alcoholics Anonymous may be a better option and would very likely be easier to find.

Gamblers Anonymous
International Service Office
P.O. Box 17173
Los Angeles, CA 90017
www.gamblersanonymous.org/
Voice: (213) 386-8789 Fax: (213) 386-0030

Sex addiction

If you cannot find a biblically based sex addiction group locally, Sexaholics Anonymous may be your best choice among national secular sex addiction groups. S.A. enforces a conservative definition of sexual sobriety: "No sexual behavior outside of a marital relationship." Another national group, Sex Addicts Anonymous, leaves it up to the participant to define sexual sobriety. Once again, you may want to attend this group in conjunction with a group like Overcomer's Outreach.

Sexaholics Anonymous
P.O. Box 111910
Nashville, TN 37222
www.sa.org
(615) 331-6230

Accountability Partners

Since working through an inpatient counseling program, Brad has learned to rely on an accountability partner to help him stay focused on recovery. Once a week Brad heads over to Starbucks. He orders a cappuccino and then sits down with a friend for a checkup session. "Have you seen anything pornographic this week?" his friend asks. After Brad responds, his friend follows up with a tougher question, "Are you lying to me?"

"I'm often tempted to lie," Brad says. "Believe me, you'll lie and try to get out of anything. It's so easy, when you're asked, to either be silent or say 'I'm doing fine.' That's human nature. But every time I've confessed I've felt so much better and was so glad that I did it and I thought, 'why did I not want to tell this?'"

The grilling sessions stay with Brad during the next week. Two or three days later, when Brad is tempted again, he thinks about the next session and knows he'll have to give an account. Maintaining an accountability partnership has been key to Brad's recovery from his struggle with pornography.

"And let us consider how we may spur one another on toward love and good deeds," the book of Hebrews tells us (Heb 10:24). God directs us to meet often with other believers in order to encourage one another. Going to church on Sunday morning is a part of that, but accountability partnerships can provide a focused outlet for spurring one another on.

Accountability relationships should be incorporated into any treatment approach. Support groups, in fact, often match participants with "sponsors," people who are further along in recovery and can act as accountability partners. Pastors and Christian counselors also recognize the role accountability plays in ongoing sobriety—especially for issues such as sexual addiction, where addicts will face continual struggles with lust.

Productive accountability relationships break the isolation of addictive behavior, provide a safe environment for confession, and extend a safety net of support. Unfortunately, faithful and compassionate accountability partners are not always easy to find—especially if you are a woman seeking help.

"Women need accountability, but they have a greater challenge finding it," says Marnie Ferree, especially when the problem is sexual in nature. "While men are growing used to talking about sexual struggles with each other, women aren't talking about sexual addiction, and many don't know how to handle the confession, recovery, or accountability process."[17]

"We women feel more shame because sex addiction is [considered] a man thing," a thirty-seven-year-old cybersex addict told Dr. Schneider. "It is not considered normal for a woman to escape her pain through sex. [That perception] made it all the harder for me to get help and admit the exact nature of my wrongs."[18]

Marnie insists, however, that accountability is an important part of a multiprong solution for women that also includes counseling and support groups. She points out that women who have a difficult time finding accountability partners could benefit from participating in a support group that would assign a sponsor to them to help with accountability. When it comes to accountability for women, Marnie says, "The earlier the better, the longer the better."[19]

Who Can Help?

If you're committed to finding an accountability partner or group, your first question may be "Whom should I ask?" If you are not aware of an accountability group at your church, your best candidates are fellow church members, friends, or relatives you trust. A gentleman named John told me how his pastor helped him find a partner. "I asked my pastor for a referral and he recommended that I evaluate the men in our church to find someone I thought I could trust with the details of my life, then ask his opinion of that person. That's what I did, and I have been meeting with my friend Rick for over a year now."

"You have to be very selective with the person you choose for accountability," Brad tells me. "It has to be a two-way street. You have to feel like you can tell them anything and they are not going to judge you, and you have to be accepting of the things they tell you. I felt like I could share anything with the guys I chose—but I couldn't do that with a lot of my friends."

"It needs to be a peer-to-peer group where there is no condescending," says Rob Jackson, president of Christians for Sexual Integrity. "If the environment is not right, it will be more injurious than helpful." Rob recommends that a man have at least three accountability partners, for effectiveness. "You can lie to one and you may be able to confuse the second, but the third may be too much to outwit."[20]

Most importantly, you need to find partners who will be committed. Benjamin shared a problem with someone in his men's Bible study and the man asked Benjamin how he could help him. "Check up on me," Benjamin said. "I wanted some accountability. If I knew he was going to ask me how I was doing it would help a lot. But he never once asked. Not once! I've become pretty good friends with him since, but we've never even broached the subject." The same thing happened with another friend in whom Benjamin confided. "In this case it was going to be mutual accountability. Even though we agreed to it, neither of us ever again said, 'so how are you doing in the sexual temptation area?'"

That's why Zach Britton, a professional colleague of mine, prayerfully considers requests to partner with someone else in accountability. "When I agree to hold someone else accountable, I feel accountable to God to do so," he says.[21] That's the kind of partner you need.

Yellow Light on Spouse

Most professionals I interviewed cautioned men not to ask their spouses to be their accountability partners. Several men I have spoken with point to a productive accountability relationship with their wives, but those men tend to be fairly healthy at this point and are generally more honest than the average recovering addict.

"What you don't want is for your wife to be your parole officer," says Dr. Schaumburg. "You need to be able to maintain an equal partnership and that's not what the parole officer and parolee relationship is. Besides, you are less likely to be totally candid with your wife about all your thoughts and actions." Schaumburg observes that guys may share their general goals with their wives, but that their wives may not be able to handle all the details of confession and full accountability.[22]

Rob Jackson recommends that the wife be an adjunct accountability partner—someone who can join the process but is not a direct participant. He suggests that she focus on the general direction of recovery and restoration of the relationship and then sign off on accountability partners for her husband, men she can contact when she has concerns.

In her role, she may want to take advantage of tools to review her husband's Internet activity, but she should not move into the role of a detective who is constantly trying to dig up clues. Her most effective focus is on restoring relationship—watching for improvements in the areas of communication and intimacy.[23]

Format for Men

So, what should an accountability relationship include? Once you have found a trustworthy partner or a group, you should commit to regular meetings where you will ask each other tough questions. "Rick and I meet for breakfast on the same day every week," says John. "We have made it a priority and now we wouldn't miss our time together for anything."

Most of the professionals I talk to recommend that guys give their accountability partners a list of at least five questions that are specific to their struggle, whether it be on-line pornography, day-trading, on-line gambling, or any other abusive activity. Their partners should ask those questions and in return provide a list of questions to be asked of them.

To provide more context for their particular questions, guys should share some of the story behind their struggle. John found this to be a scary but necessary step. "How can Rick hold me accountable or encourage me in my Christian walk if he doesn't know the temptations I face?" John asks. "It doesn't have to all come out at once, but you should feel more willing to share as the relationship grows and trust is developed."

Each session must include an honest and inquisitive run-through of the key questions—probing the areas of temptation and sin. "Sometimes we may not want to ask the same questions or probe the same areas we did the week before," says John, "but it is important that we do. Our accountability partner is counting on us to do just that."

"We are very detailed in our conversation," says Brad, "and we tell everything we do without watering it down."

Emerging technology provides accountability partners a service that makes them even more transparent to each other. A product called CyberSentinel (available at www.securitysoft.com) can send an email to an accountability partner every time you try to go to an inappropriate Web site. A similar product called Covenant Eyes (available at www.covenanteyes.org) sends a regular report to an accountability partner with a flag beside any questionable sites. Partners can use these resources as a part of their weekly review, but also as an extra wall of protection in the moment of temptation.

Any effective accountability relationship must be able to accommodate a confession of failure. "There have been times I have failed in my journey to avoid temptation," says John. "When this happens, I am ashamed and hesitant to admit my failure to Rick, let alone God. But God understands, [and] so does Rick, who gently reminds me of my goal to serve Christ and overcome temptation." John doesn't want his partner to go soft on him when he slips. "After I confess, if someone would tell me, 'that's OK, don't worry about it,' that wouldn't cut it for me," he says. "I want someone to be encouraging and loving, but to give me some motivation to not let it happen again."

Finally, a healthy accountability session requires prayer. John knows that his struggle requires strength beyond what he and his partner have together. His favorite Scripture is an apt reminder: "For our struggle is not against flesh and blood, but against the rulers, against the authorities, against the powers of this dark world and against the spiritual forces of evil in the heavenly realms" (Eph 6:12).

Chapter Nine

Addressing Behavior

Addictive behavior often begins with simple actions that become habitual and then snowball into out-of-control behavior. Simple actions leading to good habits can serve an important role in the recovery process. Two important action areas for recovery include the steps you take today to diffuse your problem and then the steps you take later to create a healthy environment for future Internet use.

Diffusing the Problem

To truly overcome an Internet addiction, you will need to spend time understanding how your thoughts, emotions, and unresolved spiritual conflicts drive your addictive behavior. To get to a place where you can reflect on those influences, however, you need to first take specific steps to eliminate harmful behavior ... today. Think of your situation as a car wreck. Your injuries will likely need long-term treatment, and they could include internal injuries. Before medics will go there, however, they will work to stop the bleeding and to get you stabilized first.

Your first step is to delete any accounts, special downloads, or profiles that you have created in order to indulge your addiction—especially if you have been hiding them from your friends and family. Remove programs for games that have gotten out of control, profiles used in chat rooms, accounts created for gambling or day-trading, and other arrangements that directly fuel your addiction. You should also set up a filtered Internet service as soon as possible and make sure that the filter is capable of keeping you away from the areas with which you struggle. There is more information about filters toward the end of this chapter.

Another way to stop the bleeding is by initiating a period of abstinence from the Internet. If you do not have to be on-line for work or other important reasons, you should try to go ninety days without being on the Internet at all. If you absolutely have to be on-line, you should work to abstain from your trouble areas. Your long-term goal will be to slowly return to moderated Internet use, but it can be difficult to go straight from abusive to moderated use. In ninety days of abstinence you can move from withdrawal pangs to control and perhaps even a total loss of appetite for the on-line experience you craved.

Creating a Safe Environment for Healthy On-Line Use

As you complete a period of abstinence from the Internet and as you take steps to work on the other areas of recovery—mental, emotional, and spiritual—you can start planning a return to healthy on-line use. After developing abusive Internet habits, just sitting down to your computer can trigger temptations to fall back into old patterns. For that reason, some people who recognize a serious problem in their life decide to go off-line indefinitely or even to get rid of their computers. In some cases, that kind of long-term abstinence is necessary. The majority of people I have known with problems, however, need their computer and Internet service for work, education, or other family necessities. Instead of total abstinence from the

Internet, they have decided to create a safe environment, so that the time they are on-line will be spent on healthy use.

Creating a safe environment is an important part of a comprehensive recovery process that depends on a genuine desire for restoration and that focuses on the deeper heart issues influencing behavior. Detached from the overall strategy, these recommendations cannot be ultimately successful.

A safe on-line environment requires four things: a commitment to purposeful Internet use, a game plan for balanced time of use, technological tools to maintain healthy boundaries, and creative approaches for temptation management.

Establishing a Purpose and Staying Focused

Why do you need the Internet? What practical purposes does it serve for you or your family? Time management guru Stephen Covey encourages his readers to develop personal or family mission statements for life.[1] You could go a step further by developing an on-line mission statement for yourself or your family. Here's the one my family adopted:

> *Our family will primarily use the Internet to meet practical needs: to conduct business, to research, to get news updates, to make planned purchases, to coordinate travel plans, and to keep in touch with friends and family. We will use technology to filter pornography, gambling, illegal activities, and other content that is not appropriate. We will make every attempt to be on-line only while family members are present and to balance Internet use with other family activities. We will raise our children to respect the opportunities and risks that the Internet provides.*

Once you have a clear purpose for your Internet use, it is important to remove temptations that undermine your purpose, and establish priorities that enforce it. If your purpose is to limit email use to valuable correspondence, then you can take steps to eliminate wasteful mail—either by unsubscribing from email groups you no longer find valuable or by using tools that sort your email according to your preferences. If your purpose is to cut back on recreational Internet use, you could review any remaining files you have downloaded for on-line games or message services to determine if they need to be deleted as well. If you are trying to put on-line relationships behind you, then you should not only eliminate profiles you have created, but also pictures you have posted to the network and memberships from any questionable clubs or newsgroups that you may have joined.

Balancing Time

As I mentioned at the beginning of the book, the Internet changes our concept of time, either by pulling us toward unlimited content without markers indicating passage of time or by compelling us to take advantage of content that is available around the clock. Developing healthy time management requires reversing these two perceptions. To do that you will need to establish a set schedule and then build in obvious time markers.

Start by setting a schedule for your week where you fill in time blocks for work or classes, church and devotions, meals, adequate sleep, exercise, and time for friends and family first. Then add in small blocks of time for checking email, sports scores, news, and whatever else you have identified as healthy Internet uses. Try to schedule those blocks of time around other activities that cannot be delayed, such as work, classes, or regular meetings.

If you have struggled with secret Internet habits, then you should make every effort to limit your Internet slots to times when other people will be around and to cut out late-night slots or other times that you recognize as temptation points. Once you have established your schedule, share it with family members or roommates and ask them to help you stick to it. Communicate with them if you ever have to make exceptions to your schedule.

Once you have your schedule, you need to take steps to hold yourself to it and also to make the passage of time more obvious while on-line. If you have scheduled Internet time from 7:00 to 7:30 P.M., you should use some kind of alarm clock (on your watch, your computer, or your desktop) that will sound when your time is up, and then you need to honor that alarm. If you have trouble maintaining your schedule, you can use software such as Cyber Patrol to limit Internet access to specific times of day.

Tools for Healthy Boundaries

You're probably aware that several new technologies have emerged for filtering, blocking, and monitoring Internet content. Maybe you've considered such a tool in the past but thought it would be too clumsy or might even be ineffective. Fortunately, the market for protective Internet technology has steadily improved over the past couple of years. Unfortunately, no technology is 100 percent effective, especially if you work hard enough to get around it. Technology alone cannot solve a problem that grows out of your heart, but it can help.

The greatest benefit of using blocking, monitoring, or filtering technology is that it reverses the illusion of convenience that causes addictive problems to grow in the first place. It does that by making it much harder to access objectionable Internet areas—pornography, gambling, chat rooms, and so forth. Several services also allow users to customize their filter to block additional areas such as games, auctions, trading services, and other sites that may have become problem areas. Some services also include filtered email—an important tool for eliminating spam mail for porn, gambling sites, or other temptations.

Protective technology can either be installed directly on your computer or be built into the service offered by your Internet provider. Service that is filtered by your provider is much harder to get around and requires less maintenance. Software installed on your computer, however, provides greater customization and generally includes additional tools for managing on-line time and outgoing information. The most comprehensive approach includes service filtered by the provider and managed by the user via computer software.

As a reviewer of various Internet safety technologies, I strongly recommend that you do some research before signing up for a service. Some services work only on 56K modems; others don't work with Macs. Also, some dial-up services aren't available outside of large metropolitan areas or fail to include convenient tech support. A good resource for finding the service that best meets your needs is the Web site Get Net Wise (www.getnetwise.org). At that site, you can complete a quick form explaining what you need in a service and then receive a customized list of services that best meet your criteria. Recently, a couple of ministries, including the National Coalition for the Protection of Children and Families as well as Focus on the Family, worked together to produce a similar resource for the Christian community called Filter Review (www.filterreview.com).

Finding the right service may require some effort on your part, but it's imperative that you take that effort to find protective technology today.

Temptation Management

Regardless of the work you do to establish purposeful Internet use, to regulate your time, and to use technology to create good boundaries, you will still face temptation. You will be tempted to fudge on your schedule or even to try to get around your filter. Creating a healthy environment for Internet use has to take into account the fact that the enemy will plague you with temptation to fall back into old patterns.

Fighting temptation is first and foremost a spiritual battle, and God promises to help us stand up to it. "No temptation has seized you except what is common to man," Paul wrote to the church at Corinth, "And God is faithful; he will not let you be tempted beyond what you can bear. But when you are tempted, he will also provide a way out so that you can stand up under it" (1 Cor 10:13).

One way to fight temptation on-line is to say a prayer every time you boot up your computer, asking God to help you avoid sin and to use the Internet in a way that glorifies him. You can enforce that prayer by playing Christian music in the background while you are on-line.

When God gave the Israelites instructions for holy living, he told them to incorporate his teachings into their lives in very practical ways: "Talk about them when you sit at home and when you walk along the road, when you lie down and when you get up. Tie them as symbols on your hands and bind them on your foreheads. Write them on the doorframes of your houses and on your gates" (Dt 6:7-9).

How can you apply that principle to your computer area? Some men I have spoken with have taped Scriptures beside their computer or used them as computer wallpaper or screensavers. The Psalms and Proverbs especially are filled with good reminders. Here are some of my favorites:

Psalm 19:14: May the words of my mouth and the meditation of my heart be pleasing in your sight, O Lord, my Rock and my Redeemer.

Psalm 101:3: I will set before my eyes no vile thing.

Proverbs 5:21: A man's ways are in full view of the Lord, and he examines all his paths.

John Erickson tells me that Ephesians 6:10-11 is a key passage for him:

Ephesians 6:10-11: Finally, be strong in the Lord and in his mighty power. Put on the full armor of God so that you can take your stand against the devil's schemes.

"Putting on the whole armor of God is vital to overcoming temptation," John says. "It is a commandment with promise—we will withstand evil (have the strength to avoid temptation), and having done everything, we will stand (overcome)." John tells me that in addition to posting verses of encouragement on his computer, he tries not to use the computer late at night or when he is alone at home. He also calls an accountability partner whenever he wrestles with temptation.

The suggestions here focus on the time you are at your computer. Temptation, however, can start anywhere. Your first line of defense is your heart. When you commit to personal purity, you learn to fight temptations as soon as they start. That's especially true for pornography. "Pornography is driven by lust—and it all starts in the mind," says Brad. "You have to stop it there; you can't let your mind dwell on it and allow it to push you toward acting out." The same can be said for gambling, interactive games, or whatever you struggle with. You can't wait until you get to your computer to start fighting those temptations.

Chapter Ten

Addressing Head and Heart

"Examine my heart and my mind," David says to God in Psalm 26:2. What would an examination of your heart and mind show? Before any addictive behavior can start, it has to bubble up out of your day-to-day thoughts and deep-seated emotions.

Dr. Kimberly Young, Dr. Maressa Orzack, Dr. Al Cooper, and other pioneers of Internet addiction research recommend cognitive therapy for treatment. Cognitive therapy recognizes that harmful patterns of thinking drive addictive behavior, and therefore addicts can move toward recovery by working to understand and change those harmful thought patterns. The concept of changing your thought life is consistent with Romans 12:2, where Paul writes, "Do not conform any longer to the pattern of this world, but be transformed by the renewing of your mind. Then you will be able to test and approve what God's will is—his good, pleasing and perfect will."

Dr. Harry Schaumburg, Dr. Steve Earll, Rob Jackson, and other Christian counselors also stress the need to address unresolved emotional conflicts when treating an addiction. Attachment disorders, trauma, relational disappointment, and other forms of emotional conflicts can feed destructive thoughts and behaviors. "Above all else, guard your heart, for it is the wellspring of life," says Proverbs 4:23, reminding us of the importance of a healthy heart.

Identifying Mental Triggers

What are you usually thinking before you go on-line, and then how do you feel when you are using your favorite Internet applications? Could there be a pattern? Addiction experts think so. In a 1980 study of multiple addictions, researchers found that negative emotional states, interpersonal conflict, or social pressure preceded 71 percent of the relapses studied.[1] The most common mental triggers spell the acronym HALT: hunger, anger, loneliness, and tiredness.

Addictions counselors often encourage clients to make an effort to observe their frame of mind around the time they feel driven to be on-line, in order to discern loneliness, depression, a need for control, or other emotions. "Paying attention to their internal world also helps clients see that there are identifiable causes as well as reinforcers for their behaviors and therefore it is something they have the potential to be able to control," says a study led by Dr. Al Cooper.[2]

The goal of identifying triggers is to help you intervene when you cognitively recognize a triggering state of mind. "Discovering the triggers to temptation was especially helpful," says John. "In my case, anxiety, depression, or a feeling of failure in other areas of my life encouraged my mind to 'punish itself' by sinning. It was important for me to know what state of mind I was in, or what activity I did, that set me up for temptation, so I could avoid it."

John's approach of reviewing his state of mind at the point of temptation is similar to the manner in which binge-eating is often treated. Binge-eaters are encouraged to identify the points of depression or anxiety over negative self-images that prompt their acting out. The treatment for Internet addiction is similar to that for eating disorders, in that Internet addicts often cannot afford to cut the Internet out of their lives any more than food addicts can afford to quit eating. "People with eating disorders can't stop eating, but they could stop eating sugar. People today can't stop working with computers and the Internet, but they could stop with the games [and other problems]," says Hilarie Cash, cofounder of Internet/Computer Addiction Services in Redmond.[3]

Since a growing majority of Americans are finding the Internet to be an important and practical part of their lives, moderation of use is more practical than total abstinence. For the most part, Internet addicts can learn to recognize triggers to binge Internet use and then develop habits that limit them to moderated use.

It's important to clarify that while addicts can work toward moderation of general Internet use, some things, like pornography and gambling, are not simply good things abused, but are toxins in and of themselves. Someone with an eating disorder can moderate his or her use of normal food, but that person's body will not tolerate him or her eating things that are poisonous. Pornography and gambling can be poisonous, and therefore need to be avoided altogether.

Some Examples of Unresolved Emotional Conflict

Mental triggers such as hunger, anger, loneliness, and other conditional situations can be fairly easy to identify and respond to. Unresolved emotional conflicts, the other underlying feeder of addictions, tend to be more deeply rooted and typically require professional guidance to work through. To identify unresolved emotional conflicts, counselors will likely touch on your relationships—with God, with your friends, with your immediate family, with the family you were born into, and even with yourself.

Dr. Schaumburg sees the issues that cause addictive behavior as an attempt to deal with relational disappointments while growing up as well as from current relationships. "First off, a person growing up is going to experience relational disappointment with their parents," says Dr. Schaumburg. "Everyone has his or her own story—either a father who died or was too busy as a pastor. They also could have had disappointment among peers—they didn't have friends or were always the last one to be picked for the baseball team."[4]

Dr. Steve Fetrow says that his clients often tell him they were raised by godly parents—people who called themselves Christians and went to church—but on closer inspection there were quite a few unresolved problems. "Men, especially, often have a defense mechanism whereby they gloss over bad areas in their relationship with their parents that need to be addressed," says Dr. Fetrow. "When relationships don't work, it hurts and we are committed as human beings to protect ourselves from pain, and so it's easier to blow it off, say it's no big deal, instead of recognizing a major rift in a relationship that has caused pain that needs to be addressed."[5]

Disappointment can also be found in current relationships. A single person may still be struggling to develop meaningful relationships with friends or a significant other. Dr. Schaumburg believes marriage creates many opportunities for disappointment—both in day-to-day relationships and in what does or doesn't happen in the bedroom.

As I mentioned earlier in the book, Dr. Schaumburg ties relational disappointment to the fall of man, and how that causes us all to bring imperfections into our relationships. Having meaningful connections in a fallen world requires honesty, forgiveness, and unconditional love. The temptation is to bypass that effort and find some kind of relational satisfaction from a less complicated delivery system—pornography, an on-line affair, or a fantasy game. "You can just click and point to deal with relational disappointment now," he says.[6]

Steve Earll, an addictions counselor, specializes in the area of family trauma. He points out that unhealthy responses to various forms of family trauma can make someone vulnerable to addictions. He consistently finds some kind of unresolved trauma in either current families or birth families for the clients he sees.

"The first area is parental loss—either from a major illness, abandonment, death, or divorce or from the distance caused by various addictions to alcohol, drugs, and sex and even addictions to work and food." Other traumas, such as emotional, physical, verbal, or sexual abuse, can leave deeper scars. Almost everyone deals with some kind of trauma in his or her lifetime, Steve says, but health comes from going through a grieving process to deal with it—adequately addressing the loss and moving on.

"Trauma will be dealt with one way or the other—either toward health or dysfunction," he says. "Dysfunction occurs when people fail to work through a healthy grieving process and instead create rules for self-protection."[7]

Claudia Black details those rules in her book, *Double Duty*:

1. Don't trust other people: you can't be sure about security and love—who can you really trust?
2. Don't feel your emotions: deny them, change them, or stuff them away so that you are not vulnerable.
3. Don't talk about what's real and significant: if you don't bring the problem up again, it's taken care of.
4. Control and manipulate others so that you can still have

your relational needs met: set up situations with expectations and always attach strings to them. Control and manipulation can either be active—in your face and direct—or passive—guerilla warfare where you say one thing and do the opposite.[8]

"We apply these rules into new relationships," says Steve Earll. "The unspoken message is 'Let's get these rules straight, I don't trust you, I don't want to talk about my feelings, and I want to be in control.'" As a result, shame, fear, loneliness, anger, and other emotions boil up in this process and become a breeding ground for addictions. "The addiction seems to meet needs easier than a relationship," he says. "With the addiction, there is no need for trust, expression of emotions, or any other violations of the rules."[9]

Chapter Eleven

Restoring Relationship With God

Have you, like Brad in his struggle with pornography, cried out to God for help? Did he seem far away, unable to help you regain control in your life?

Addictive habits have a way of blurring your understanding of God and can make it difficult for you to receive his help in recovery. Maybe your relationship with God is blocked by spiritual conflicts. Maybe you are having trouble trusting that God still loves you and is capable of forgiving and restoring you. Maybe you don't understand why God doesn't just restore you instantaneously. This chapter looks at the concepts of resolving spiritual conflicts, experiencing God's forgiveness, and understanding how he guides restoration.

Resolving Spiritual Conflicts

Addictions counselor Rob Jackson encourages clients to answer four questions about God:

"What do I know about God?"

"How do I feel about God?"

"What do I know and feel about my parents, and how have I projected that onto God?"

"Do I enjoy God?"

The answers to these questions can often help him to identify unresolved spiritual conflicts that can in turn feed addictions.

Among the conflicts he identifies are: an emphasis on religion over relationship, a lack of spiritual discipline, a focus on external performance, compartmentalization of secret sin, the projection of family problems onto God, and a failure to attach to God.[1]

Rob tells me that the longer he spends time treating problems like sex addiction, the more he sees the importance of restoring an addict's understanding of God's unconditional love. "At his core, an addict has an intimacy disorder—a problem opening up and connecting deeply with other people," he says. "That also includes his relationship with God." Often addicts have a distorted view of their heavenly Father's love because the love they received from their father was so far from ideal or because their cultural view of God's love fell short. Rob goes on to explain that when addicts hit a bad place, they have a tendency to "put God on trial" because they see him as some nebulous power instead of as a loving Father who sacrificed his Son for them.[2]

Experiencing Forgiveness

King David demonstrated how easy it is for godly men to fall, and then he modeled how we should approach God for restoration (see 2 Sm 12 and Ps 51).

There he was, looking out from his palace, surveying all the blessings and responsibilities God had given him. Then he saw a woman bathing. David could have looked away. But he crossed a line and sent someone to find out about her. The man he sent reported that it was Bathsheba, the wife of Uriah, one of David's soldiers. David could have asked God to help him deal with his lust for a married woman, but he crossed another line and had Bathsheba brought to him. He slept with her.

When Bathsheba sent word that she was pregnant, David started working to hide his sin. He tried to get Uriah to come home from fighting and to sleep with his wife. When that didn't work, he made arrangements for Uriah to be killed in battle. Finally, Nathan the prophet confronted David and showed him the extent of his sin. At that point, David cried out to God.

Throughout the Psalms, David's words to God—whether in praise or pleading—help us to articulate our own feelings to God. Psalm 51 is specifically David's prayer to God following his sin with Bathsheba, but it serves as a model of confession and repentance for all of us:

> Have mercy on me, O God, according to your unfailing love; according to your great compassion blot out my transgressions. Wash away all my iniquity and cleanse me from my sin. For I know my transgressions, and my sin is always before me. Against you, you only, have I sinned and done what is evil in your sight, so that you are proved right when you speak and justified when you judge. Surely I was sinful at birth, sinful from the time my mother conceived me. Surely you desire truth in the inner parts; you teach me wisdom in the inmost place. Cleanse me with hyssop, and I will be clean; wash me, and I will be whiter than snow. Let me hear joy and gladness; let the bones you have crushed rejoice. Hide your face from my sins and blot out all my iniquity. Create in me a pure heart, O God, and renew a steadfast spirit within me. Do not cast me from your presence or take your Holy Spirit from me. Restore to me the joy of your salvation and grant me a willing spirit, to sustain me. Then I will teach transgressors your ways, and sinners will turn back to you.

Save me from bloodguilt, O God, the God who saves me, and my tongue will sing of your righteousness. O Lord, open my lips, and my mouth will declare your praise. You do not delight in sacrifice, or I would bring it; you do not take pleasure in burnt offerings. The sacrifices of God are a broken spirit; a broken and contrite heart, O God, you will not despise.

PSALM 51:1-17

David's prayer is a guide that models four fundamental steps for breaking free from sin and restoring relationship with God: recognizing our fallen nature, understanding how our sin is against God, confessing with a repentant heart, and asking God for mercy and a restored relationship.

David Recognized His Fallen Nature

"Surely I was sinful at birth, sinful from the time my mother conceived me," David says in verse 5. David recognized that he was born with a sinful nature. Of course, we were all born like David; Romans 3:23 says, "For all have sinned and fall short of the glory of God." It can be tempting to call sin something else—to see it as just a weakness or a character flaw. Dr. Steve Fetrow believes that people with addictive problems don't focus enough on what it means to be fallen people who live in a fallen world.

"We're fallen people in a fallen world—that's a nice statement," Dr. Fetrow says, "but what does it really mean? How does that play out in your life—in your relationships with your spouse, your parents, your kids? We need to camp there. We need to take a hard look at our sin and wickedness. We don't struggle and wrestle with that enough."[3]

David Recognized That His Sin Was Against God

In verse 4, David says, "Against you, you only, have I sinned and done what is evil in your sight, so that you are proved right when you speak and justified when you judge." David recognized that while his sin had hurt others, his transgression was against God.

The book of James tells us "each one is tempted when, by his own evil desire, he is dragged away and enticed. Then, after desire has conceived, it gives birth to sin; and sin, when it is full-grown, gives birth to death" (Jas 1:14-15).

King David's sin started with an innocent glance, mushroomed, and then led to death. Yet the death was not just that of Uriah, or even of the son that Bathsheba bore; it was death in the relationship that David had once shared with God. When Nathan the prophet confronted him, David admitted, "I have sinned against the Lord" (2 Sm 12:13).

The Old Testament warns against the worship of idols in the place of God. Few people today worship carved statues, yet we may not realize how easily the pleasures we seek out become our idols—how we tend to worship those things instead of God.

"Once we give our desire for life to any object other than God, we become ensnared," says author and counselor John Eldredge. "We become slaves to any number of things, which at the outset we thought would serve us."[4]

In an earlier book, John's cowriter, Brent Curtis, explains why the things we try to place in areas reserved for God end up enslaving us:

We put our hope in meeting a lover who will give us some form of immediate gratification, some taste of transcendence that will place a drop of water on our parched tongue. This taste of transcendence, coming as it does from a nontranscendent source, whether that be an affair, a drug, an obsession with sports, pornography, or living off of our giftedness, has the same effect on our souls as crack cocaine. Because the gratification touches us in that heart-place made for transcendent communion, without itself being transcendent, it attaches itself to our desire with chains that render us captive.[5]

It grieves God's heart to see us settle for what Curtis describes as "nontranscendent sources," because he knows the bondage and emptiness that follow.

David Confessed With a Repentant Heart

In verse 3, David says, "For I know my transgressions, and my sin is always before me." Later, in verses 16 and 17, he adds, "You do not delight in sacrifice, or I would bring it; you do not take pleasure in burnt offerings. The sacrifices of God are a broken spirit; a broken and contrite heart, O God, you will not despise."

David admitted his sinfulness and approached God with a contrite, or sorrowfully repentant, heart. Any change requires confession to God and seriousness about turning away from the sin.

In the New Testament, James writes, "Therefore confess your sins to each other and pray for each other so that you may be healed. The prayer of a righteous man is powerful and effective" (Jas 5:16). "Only when I became humble, confessed, and started to seek God's face, did I start to change," says Craig, a man who maintained a pattern of sexual sin despite being caught several times and getting arrested.[6]

"Confession knocks down the façade—it takes off the mask," says Dr. Fetrow. "It allows us to say, 'I'm a mess.' Confession helps people to grapple with who they really are."[7] Instead of working to show God how we can fix our problem, God desires us to approach him as we are, with repentant hearts.

David knew he could do nothing in his own strength to make things right. No sacrifice on his part could replace what God most wanted from him—a broken and contrite heart. When you have grown dependent on an Internet experience you may think you are still in control, that you could stop your behavior if you had to. Yet your short-lived resolutions and half steps toward fixing the problem are in some ways like the burnt offerings in which God finds no pleasure.

"It was a big revelation to me that there was no way I could fight the problem myself," Brad said about his porn struggle. "I knew that I needed God's strength." When he finally gave up on his attempts to handle his problem alone, and simply approached God with brokenness, Brad was able to see a change.

David Asked God for Mercy and for a Renewed Relationship
"Have mercy on me, O God, according to your unfailing love; according to your great compassion blot out my transgressions," David cried out. "Wash away all my iniquity and cleanse me from my sin.... Cleanse me with hyssop, and I will be clean; wash me, and I will be whiter than snow" (Ps 51:1-2, 7).

"Hide your face from my sins and blot out all my iniquity," he added. "Create in me a pure heart, O God, and renew a steadfast spirit within me. Do not cast me from your presence or take your Holy Spirit from me. Restore to me the joy of your salvation and grant me a willing spirit, to sustain me" (Ps 51:9-12).

David knew he needed a clean slate. He asked God to show mercy and compassion by cleansing him from sin. Most importantly, he asked God to create in him a pure heart and to give him a steadfast spirit. If you have filled your mind with perverse sexual images or shared depraved thoughts with someone else on-line, then you may especially appreciate an opportunity to be washed whiter than snow—to have God begin to restore your innocence.

John the beloved explains the promise we have following Jesus' sacrifice for us: "If we confess our sins, he is faithful and just and will forgive us our sins and purify us from all unright-eousness" (1 Jn 1:9).

God's incredible willingness to extend forgiveness to us, no matter how shameful or selfish we have been, is tied to the unconditional love he extends to us. A consistent message I hear from addictions counselors is that their clients long to be known and loved deeply but have difficulty allowing anyone to get close enough to love them that way. They suspect that no one would love them completely if they knew what they were really like. Their addiction, in turn, becomes a place to escape for something like love without the same vulnerability.

The great truth that can set you free is that God does know you—all the good and all the bad—yet he loves you completely. John the beloved goes on to explain how God's love removes our sin: "This is love: not that we loved God, but that he loved us and sent his Son as an atoning sacrifice for our sins" (1 Jn 4:10).

Struggle and Steps Toward Renewal

Recovery begins when you recognize your problem and con-fess it to God with a repentant heart. At that point he can for-give you and begin restoration. Often there can be amazing results when addicts follow David's example by recognizing that they have a problem and submitting completely to God.

Through his supernatural power, God can break chains of spiritual bondage. While God is capable of working miraculously, he often works methodically, leading us through periods of self-discovery and relationship restoration.

"When it comes to major problems, we ask God for wisdom, we turn it over to God, and then we wrestle, with God's leading and his guidance," says addictions counselor Steve Earll. "If it is oppression, it will be taken away. If you pray for deliverance and you are not delivered, however, then with God's strength and guidance, you get down to work. I know people who God has chosen to take their desires away and then others who seemed to have just as much faith but God lets them wrestle with their problem. I believe God says, 'my grace is sufficient, roll up your sleeves and get down to it.'"[8]

Steve finds inspiration for this struggle in the opening verses of the book of James:

> Consider it pure joy, my brothers, whenever you face trials of many kinds, because you know that the testing of your faith develops perseverance. Perseverance must finish its work so that you may be mature and complete, not lacking anything. If any of you lacks wisdom, he should ask God, who gives generously to all without finding fault, and it will be given to him.
>
> JAMES 1:2-5

The payoff for this struggle is made clear a few verses later: "Blessed is the man who perseveres under trial, because when he has stood the test, he will receive the crown of life that God has promised to those who love him" (Jas 1:12).

Simple behavior modifications will not be successful in the long run if you don't take your struggle to God and allow him to guide the process and work on your heart. After taking that foundational step you can begin to take practical steps to remove temptation and to demonstrate accountability for time and effort.

At that point, you are not alone in your efforts. You are not working in your own strength; you are demonstrating obedience to God and developing habits of integrity in the place of habits of compromise.

"When recovery is done spiritually, out of restored relationship with God, it guides the whole process," says Rob Jackson. "Your emotions can be freed, your thought life can be renewed, and behavioral change can come with obedience to God's commands."[9]

Perhaps you have never known God as a loving Father. Rediscovering his incredible love and compassion for you will be of much greater benefit than just breaking an addictive habit. If you have fallen away from a close relationship with God, this is the time to once again experience a clean heart and to enjoy again the walks and talks with God in the cool of the day.

Chapter Twelve

Practical Steps for the Person Concerned

Brenda's heart ached. Her husband, a youth pastor, had been arrested. The problem behind it all was even worse than the arrest itself—he had an uncontrollable sexual addiction.

Frank didn't see it coming. His job kept him on the road a lot, but he thought his relationship with his wife—a Sunday school teacher—was fine. He didn't know his wife's casual conversations about religion in a Christian chat room had grown into an affair, until she announced she was leaving him.

For Brenda and for Frank, these situations were tragedies. They felt hurt, betrayed, and helpless. Yet they made it. The good news is that today their relationships are restored and are continually improving. The process was difficult and required incredible patience and forgiveness on their part. It also required a lot of vulnerability and willingness to look at their own lives. Still, they'll both tell you that their commitment to recovery paid off.

Are you facing a similar tragedy? Are you still in shock after finding a stash of on-line porn, discovering that your husband's day-trading has wiped out your savings account, or hearing that your wife has lost her job for constantly violating company policies against personal Internet use?

Or are you just becoming concerned about where your spouse's on-line habits are headed? Has your spouse's daily on-line time grown from a few minutes into a few hours? Is he on-line later and later into the night? Is she increasingly irritable when you question her Internet use?

Whether your spouse is just starting to show signs of excessive Internet use or has allowed a habit to explode in some tragic way, I encourage you to fight for your relationship. You have every reason to care about the health of your marriage and to take appropriate steps to keep the Internet from driving a wedge between you and your spouse.

The tough challenge for you at this point is to direct your thoughts and emotions in a positive direction. That's difficult when you feel hurt, anxious, and vulnerable. Dr. James Dobson addresses this struggle in his book *Love Must be Tough*: "As a love affair begins to deteriorate, the vulnerable partner is inclined to panic. Characteristic responses include grieving, lashing out, begging, pleading, grabbing and holding; or the reaction may be just the opposite, involving appeasement and passivity." Dr. Dobson says such reactions are understandable but are not often successful in restoring the relationship. "In fact," he says, "such reactions are usually counterproductive, destroying the relationship the threatened person is trying so desperately to preserve."[1]

So, what do you do? You start with prayer and follow with a day-to-day commitment to love your spouse the way God loves you. The purpose of this chapter is to give you some general direction, to answer some of the questions that are likely to be going through your mind, and to direct you to resources that can help you understand and address the struggle your marriage is facing.

What If I Only Suspect a Problem?

A large majority of the population uses the Internet on a frequent basis without having a problem. Additionally, millions of Internet surfers are able to limit their use of on-line auction services, stock-trading services, interactive games, and even chat rooms to healthy, productive purposes. It is also typical for many Internet users to go through periods of something like an initial interest binge, either when they first go on-line or when they discover a new resource, and spend several hours exploring it.

What you should be worried about are signs that your spouse's use is getting out of control—excessive time on-line that takes him or her away from family, chores, and other responsibilities; irritability or anger when asked about on-line activity or asked to get off-line; or financial irregularities and other dramatic changes in routine or behavior.

Additional signs may accompany a secret pornography habit or other on-line sexual activity, says Dr. Kimberly Young, a pioneer in Internet addiction research. She encourages spouses to look for changes in sleep patterns, demands for privacy, evidence of lying, personality changes, a loss of interest in sex, and a declining investment in the marriage.[2]

One way to determine if your spouse's activity is drifting off into inappropriate areas is to simply ask him or her, "What are you doing while you are on-line?" If your spouse seems defensive or deceptive, you may want to get a more accurate idea by reviewing the history files on your browser. If you have Microsoft Explorer, just click the "History" button near the top of the page. In newer versions of Netscape Explorer, you can find a history option under the "Communicator" category. For older versions, just enter the phrase "about:global" into the address box and press enter. If you have version 4.0 or later of America Online, you can just click the arrow to the right hand side of your locator bar to see what AOL and web files have been viewed recently.

The history file usually provides documentation for the

locations and times of all Web traffic over the past month or so. A history file that is empty or has only a couple of files in it despite a lot of recent activity may be an indication that your spouse has found out how to clear the browser history (an option available in the preferences area of the browser). Your spouse may not be aware, however, that pictures from the Web sites they visit are usually stored in a temporary area called a cache file. You can usually find that file on both PCs and Mac computers by using the "Find" feature and doing a search among file folders with the words "cache" or "webcache." This folder will bring up a list of item names with the suffix ".gif" or ".jpg." By clicking on those file names, you can see what pictures have been downloaded. If you see either pornography or gambling-related images, then you know that someone in your house has a problem that needs to be addressed.

Should I Confront My Spouse?

If you see indications that your spouse's Internet use is out of control or if you have reason to believe that he or she is involved in some form of on-line sex, gambling, or day-trading, then you need to confront him or her with your concern. You don't have to be judgmental or condemning; you should simply express with love the things that concern you and wait for your spouse's response. For example, you might say, "Honey, I feel like your on-line activities are taking you away from me and the family"; "I found some inappropriate stuff on our computer. Do you know where it came from?"; or "I love you, but I'm concerned because our marriage is in trouble, and I see the following: [detail specific problems]."

There is an outside chance that your spouse was not

responsible for the images you found or that your spouse was genuinely not aware that his or her Internet use had given you reason to be concerned. Confrontation under these circumstances is helpful because it gives you the opportunity to restore trust and open communication.

However, if you are tapping into a real problem, the response could be ugly. Out of embarrassment, your spouse may grow defensive and try to minimize the problem, or may even try to shift blame for his or her actions to you: "There wouldn't be a problem if you weren't so paranoid."

Because of the unpredictability of confrontation, many spouses choose to avoid it, even after they have seen early warning signs. Instead, they hope for the best and just try to tolerate a less fulfilling relationship. "In that case, they need to quit looking at their spouse through their eyes and see them through God's eyes," says Rob Jackson, a Christian counselor who had to fight to restore his marriage. "God doesn't want you to focus on what you would do to please your spouse. He wants you to focus on what he expects or requires of you—a very different standard." He doesn't want sin to keep someone from having an abundant life and a healthy marriage—even if the spouse is too afraid to confront the problem.

As difficult as confrontation can be and as unpredictable as the response can be, some people actually want to be caught so they can be relieved of a secret struggle. "Hopefully, your spouse is like many who get caught in the trap of addiction," says Steve Arterburn, founder of New Life Clinics. "They know what they are doing is wrong. They are aware of the sorry nature of their lives. The problem is that they don't know how to initiate changes in their behaviors. What seems most painful to you may be exactly what they need in order to begin the healing and recovery process."

"Confrontation is really your only power," says Marsha Means, an author who wrote about her husband's struggle with pornography. "You're powerless; it's up to God and that person after you confront."

How Do I Handle His/Her Denial or Refusal to Get Help?

Don't be surprised if your spouse either denies having a problem (despite your evidence) or admits having a problem but refuses to take meaningful steps to address it.

"Denial of a problem or not wanting to get help is a symptom of the real problem and if you have to wait for your spouse to say they're finally ready, they may never get there," says Dr. Harry Schaumburg, a sexual addiction counselor. Schaumburg believes your approach should be to invite them to help you improve your marriage. You could say: "this whole thing that you've been struggling with—without seeing change—has really taken its toll on me. I don't like how it affects how I feel about you. You need to do this, because I'm hurting."

If your spouse will not respond to that approach, Rob Jackson recommends that you follow the model of confrontation laid out in Matthew 18:

> If your brother sins against you, go and show him his fault, just between the two of you. If he listens to you, you have won your brother over. But if he will not listen, take one or two others along, so that "every matter may be established by the testimony of two or three witnesses."
>
> MATTHEW 18:15-16

In other words, if confronting one-on-one doesn't work, confront your spouse with witnesses: business partners, friends, or a pastor (but not your children).

"Love bomb them," says Dr. Jennifer Schneider, a researcher who wrote about her response to an adulterous husband in her book *Back from Betrayal.* She recommends a format similar to the interventions spouses often use to confront alcoholics.[3]

Rob Jackson recommends that you go into the confrontation with a treatment game plan (a support group, counseling sessions, etc.) already worked out among your witness team. If your spouse still seems reluctant to get help, you will need to say, "Here is what you are doing, here are the directives, I'm willing to get help, too. If not, you are jeopardizing the relationship to the point of separation." Rob believes this approach is important because the addict needs to work as a team player and to quit trying to be independent of the family. "No one family member is more important than the rest of the family," he says.[4]

When Is It Appropriate for Me to Leave?

Christian counselors generally agree that you should physically separate yourself from your spouse if you or your children are being exploited or victimized, or are enduring ongoing verbal abuse or emotional cruelty. You should not tolerate an environment where physical, emotional, and sexual abuse is occurring. When there is not a direct threat, however, Rob Jackson believes that separation should be the exception rather than the rule. He suggests that some women tend to minimize their husband's behavior and not recognize it as abusive. He recommends that those women go with their

hearts if they feel that their husband's actions are not cherish-
ing and have made their home unsafe.

Separation that does occur should be therapeutic, not in
anger, Rob says. He compares therapeutic separation to the
fire lines that firefighters often set to stop blazes. By inten-
tionally burning a controlled area, they can remove the threat
of a disastrous wildfire. Similarly, instead of having a problem
flare up and destroy a relationship, a brief therapeutic separation can create an environment for recovery that will hopefully keep the couple from having to go through a permanent
separation later.[5]

This process should be mediated by a pastor or counselor,
who establishes goals for what the couple will try to achieve
during their time apart. The first phase of the separation
involves thirty days with no contact between the husband and
wife. Any arrangements for finances or care for children
should be negotiated up front, so that communication can be
limited strictly to emergencies. This experience shows couples
what divorce feels like. Rob notices that couples going
through problems often have only a pseudodivorce. In such a
situation one of the partners gets kicked out of the house, but
then the two still have sex occasionally, and have long phone
calls and other kinds of on-again, off-again contact, making
recovery difficult. Total separation, however, forces the spouse
with the addiction to see what losing his or her partner completely would be like.

During this time, the husband and wife should spend time
working on individual issues with a counselor. Over the next
thirty days, the couple should start including a joint counseling session once a week. They should also add in a date night
once a week, where they spend time being civil toward each
other. By the seventh or eighth week, the couple should start

to address the kind of minimal changes that will have to occur when they come back together—no infidelity, no cybersex, and so forth.

In the last phase, the couple moves back in together, maintaining a period of joint counseling and beginning to tackle long-term issues such as communication and financial management.

My Wife Has a Cybersex Problem. What Do I Do?

The Pure Intimacy Web site I edit is divided into an area for the person who struggles with on-line sexual temptation and another area for the concerned spouse. Surprisingly, at least 25 percent of those visiting the area for the concerned spouse identify themselves as men. The emails they write tell about their wives' on-line affairs or sometimes even problems with pornography. The saddest thing about these emails is that the men are really hurt, and they don't have a clue what to do about it all.

"Because of the incredible shame they face, men are not as eager to talk through their spouse's sexual problems as women often are," says Dr. Schneider, who believes many aren't getting the help they need.[6] "Shame is greater for the husband of a sex addict, because their wife's actions go against cultural expectations," says Marnie Ferree, a marriage and family therapist. She believes it causes men to question what their wife's addiction says about their masculinity and their marriage.

According to Ferree, husbands of sex addicts typically respond in one of two ways: either they grow very controlling and angry and then refuse to take responsibility for their role in the problem, or they become very passive and try to ignore the problem.[7]

In your hurt and embarrassment, you have to find a balance between those extremes. You can't ignore the problem. You have to fight for your relationship, but you can't do it out of a sense of anger or control. You have to boldly share your concerns with your wife and then release her to God and often to professional help as well.

That's what Frank resolved to do when his wife left him for someone she met on-line. For a year, Frank prayed for his wife and continued to extend forgiveness and unconditional love as best he could despite his hurt. That was exactly what his wife needed. "Frank just amazes me with his unconditional love, and he says that ... comes [only] from God," she says, now that they are back together. "I still can't believe God gave him the strength to forgive me and not let it eat away at him and our marriage."

Frank was also willing to take the difficult step of looking at his own life to see how he could help improve his marriage. Now he encourages other men to look at underlying relational problems that may be fueling their wives' struggles. "Find out why your wife is resorting to this type of behavior," he says. "See if it is out of loneliness or not enough communication in the marriage." Once Frank realized that he had not been communicating his feelings very well, he started sending his wife emails—a format that helped him to open up. "I couldn't believe they were from my husband," his wife says. "I was so moved by what he was saying. He could never say that in person. I started falling in love with him all over again. I saw a side of him I'd never seen before."

My Spouse Is Blaming Everything on Me.
Do I Really Share Any of the Blame?

Your spouse can never justify addictive or adulterous behavior by placing the blame on you. He or she is solely responsible for whatever actions he or she has taken. Having said that, however, it is important to note that relational problems cannot occur in a vacuum. Inevitably there are vulnerabilities in the communication or intimacy you share with your spouse that need your attention. While not accepting blame from your spouse, you should be willing to reflect on your personal shortcomings within the recovery process.

Dr. Fetrow says that most couples that approach him to address sexual problems discover that each partner has issues to address. "Although one person has a presenting problem, the relationship is both people's problem," Dr. Fetrow says, "and the fact that the relationship isn't growing the way it should isn't just because one person is into pornography, but it's because there are some other relational things that aren't happening that need to be addressed as well."[8]

One way that you may unintentionally be contributing to your spouse's problem is by not confronting the problem head-on. "For an addiction to progress, the spouse has to deny and believe excuses," says Steve Earll, a Christian addictions counselor. "The lying and enabling has to stop. You must exert a strong level of truth with love, care, and concern."[9]

When it comes to sex addictions, statistical evidence shows that couples often pair up with mutual baggage to begin with. Sex addiction pioneer Patrick Carnes estimates that 81 percent of sex addicts were sexually abused at one point, and as many as 81 percent of their spouses were sexually abused before marriage as well.

"Recovery requires treating your marriage like a three-legged stool," says Rob Jackson. "Each individual represents a leg in the stool, and one of the legs represents the relationship the individuals have together." Rob says that couples don't have the luxury of building one leg at a time—they need to work on all three legs in a simultaneous recovery effort.

My Spouse Has Asked Me to Hold Him Accountable. What Should I Do?

If your spouse has recognized that he or she has a problem and has asked you for help, there are things you can do to provide encouragement and accountability. However, you should not accept the responsibility of being your spouse's only accountability partner. The best role you can play is that of an adjunct accountability partner. In that role, you can sign off on other accountability partners and oversee the recovery and restoration of your marriage.

You have the right to ask every legitimate question of your spouse that you want, but you should examine your motives. Why do you want to know? Are you trying to be controlling or punishing? Some questions are better saved for a counseling session, where the counselor can moderate how the story is disclosed and how the spouse receives it.

For questions about daily thoughts and temptations, it will be better if your spouse answers those with a same-sex accountability partner who understands a little bit more how he or she is wired. "Knowing every thought that passes through your spouse's mind is more harmful than helpful," says Marsha Means. Marsha wrote the book *Living With Your Husband's Secret Wars* after helping her husband through a porn addiction. She explains that you shouldn't let your marriage digress into a parole officer/parolee relationship.[10]

"I didn't want to be my husband's watchdog," says Brenda regarding the accountability that followed her husband's recovery. "I wanted the marriage itself to be a barometer for me for how our marriage was going. Because we were growing in intimacy and working on our communication, I watched that process instead of evidence of acting out as signs of a problem."[11]

Can Technology Help?

A simple way to provide an element of accountability in your home is to use Internet filtering technology. Whether your spouse struggles with pornography, gambling, day-trading, or another problem, filtering software can usually be customized to block access to that trouble area.

Two different filtering approaches have individual strengths. Filters that are installed directly on your computer provide tools for regulating the time of day and length of time that the Internet can be used. Often they can also monitor email, and other Internet applications. Filters that are located at your Internet service provider, however, are harder to work around, and also require less maintenance. The most protective approach involves installing software onto a computer receiving service that is filtered by your Internet provider.

Don't put all your trust in technology, however. Not only does technology have bugs every once in a while, it also cannot take the place of relationship. Filtering technology should be used within the context of a family pledge to use the Internet appropriately. In addition, your spouse should still seek out accountability partners to address lust and other temptations that technology alone cannot eliminate.

The point is that technology must be part of a comprehensive recovery approach. In her survey of spouses of sex addicts, Dr. Jennifer Schneider noticed that some spouses simply installed protective software and spent their time snooping on their mates and trying to block them from the places they tried to go on-line. She found that these efforts did not lead to long-term recovery, however, because they were "negative" in nature and not tied to "positive" recovery efforts such as marital counseling and support groups.

Information to help you find a good filtered Internet service is available at the end of this chapter.

A Friend Told Me I Was Being Too Controlling— How Much Can I Really Do?

A desire to be in control is a natural response for someone who has just been thrown into the vulnerability and instability of a damaged relationship. "Spouses want to take control and take charge," says Marsha Means. "They live in fear of what might happen, and that fuels the problem."[12] As Dr. Dobson pointed out in *Love Must be Tough*, efforts to control the recovery process can often backfire.[13]

That does not mean, however, that you should ignore the problem and sit on the sidelines. Remember that a passive response is equally inappropriate. The best route for balance between being controlling and being passive is to release control to God and then obediently follow the active steps he leads you to take. Brenda found that one aspect of releasing control to God meant that she quit trying to shield her husband from the consequences of his mistakes. "God is engineering the circumstances," she says. "We can't always protect our spouses from the consequences, and it is the consequences that may be necessary to create the brokenness and bottoming out necessary to effectively address the problem."[14]

A consistent message I hear from Christian counselors and spouses who have helped their partners through recovery is that the marriage must stay on equal footing—the concerned spouse cannot take on a parenting role. "Your goal is to remain as equals," says Marsha Means. "You want a peer relationship with mutual respect."[15]

Dr. Harry Schaumburg maintains that meaningful marriages depend on an environment of trust and respect. "A man doesn't want to go home to a wife who is standing there with her hands on her hips, saying 'OK, what did you do today? I want to check your pager and your briefcase.'" Dr. Schaumburg has one client whose wife went to work and checked his locker and then hired a detective to put a camera in his hotel room during a business trip to see if he was having an affair. "Who wants to come home to that?" Schaumburg asks.[16]

As an alternative to being controlling and doing detective work, Schaumburg encourages the concerned spouse—wives especially—to invite their partners to a restored relationship. "When you first met, to what did you invite each other? What was your relationship going to be about?" he asks wives in counseling. As the wife thinks back to simpler and more promising times, he asks her another question: "How do you take what now seems like a threatening situation, and how do you have the courage to invite him back to something you've had before?" Often, the response is, "Too much has happened since then—look at what he has done." Schaumburg's next question is, "How do you forgive him?"

The goal in Schaumburg's process is to help the couple move beyond managing the problem at hand and on to the greater task of restoring a meaningful relationship built on love and forgiveness.

What Is the First Step When My Spouse Has a Gambling or Day-Trading Problem?

Several Internet habits—emailing, general surfing, use of on-line auction services or interactive games—can be moderated and limited to healthy use. Gambling on-line and day-trading are habits that are difficult to moderate. Gambling has grown to be an acceptable vice in our country, but biblical principles regarding stewardship, greed, and love of neighbor indicate that gambling is a sin that God does not approve at any level.

Day-trading, due to its rapid action, is difficult to moderate. The Securities Exchange Commission has specifically warned investors that the practice of day-trading is incredibly risky and that only a small minority of day-traders are profitable. Traditional financial advisors recommend that investors abstain from day-trading and instead work with money managers who can supervise trading and provide valuable strategy.

For these reasons, you should take steps to help your spouse quit day-trading or gambling on-line. You should follow the guidelines mentioned earlier for appropriate confrontation and encourage your spouse to abstain from gambling or day-trading. If he or she is not able to faithfully abstain, you should make efforts to get your spouse into a treatment regimen that addresses compulsive gambling disorders.

Unfortunately, it's not always easy to discover a gambling problem, or even to find evidence of day-trading. People will often set up private accounts or secretly take money out of investment accounts. Some even embezzle money from their employers. If you only suspect a problem, there are signs you can look for, according to Dr. Valerie Lorenz, executive director of the Compulsive Gambling Center in Baltimore. She says to watch for a change in your spouse's behavior—for him or her to be argumentative, violent, and withdrawn. Watch for your spouse's work to be affected, and for him or her to be preoccupied with indebtedness.

Upon identifying a compulsive gambling problem, whether it is expressed through on-line casinos or cloaked in the practice of day-trading, Lorenz recommends that you not only seek professional help, but also take steps to eliminate the means for gambling. That means cutting off the venue for gambling as well as cutting off the supply of money. You can either use an Internet filter or temporarily go off-line to cut off the venue. To cut off the supply of money, you need to do a review of all of your accounts and consider putting everything into your name.[17]

What Resources Are Available?

Educational Web Sites

On Addictions

- Center for Online Addiction/Dr. Kimberly Young (www.netaddiction.com)
- Computer Addiction Services/ Maressa Hecht Orzack, Ph.D. (www.computeraddiction.com)
- The Center for Internet Studies (www.virtual-addiction.com)

On Sexual Intimacy Problems

- Pure Intimacy (www.pureintimacy.org)
- Passionate Commitment (www.passionatecommitment.com)

Filtering Technology

The market for Internet filtering services is as varied as the automobile market and is constantly changing. You can use one of the two following resources to find out which service is best for your particular needs:

- GetNetWise (www.getnetwise.org)
- FilterReview (www.filterreview.com)

Counseling Referral Services

Focus on the Family counseling referral service (719) 531-3400 weekdays 9:00 A.M. to 4:30 P.M. (MST); ask for the counseling department.

Christians for Sexual Integrity 500 Lake Street, Suite 105 Excelsior, MN 55344 www.sexualintegrity.org (866) 224-6838 (toll free) CSI's Call Center focuses on sexual problems. It is available between the hours of 9:00 A.M. and 5:00 P.M. (CST), Monday through Friday.

Support Groups

Please read the chapter on support groups before contacting these organizations:

Overcomer's Outreach 520 N. Brookhurst, Suite 121 Anaheim, CA 92801 (www.overcomersoutreach.org) 1-800-310-3001 or (714) 491-3000

COSA (Codependents of Sex Addicts) COSA National Service Organization (or COSA NSO) P.O. Box 14537 Minneapolis, MN 55414 cosa@shore.net (www.shore.net/~cosa) (612) 537-6904

S-Anon
A national twelve-step program
for partners and families of sex
addicts and sex offenders.
P.O. Box 111242
Nashville, TN 37222-1242
sanon@sanon.org
(www.sanon.org)
(615) 833-3152

Gambling-Anon International
Service Office, Inc.
P.O. Box 157
Whitestone, NY 11357
(www.gam-anon.org)
(718) 352-1671 phone
(718) 746-2571 fax

Intensive Counseling
Stone Gate Ministries
11509 Palmer Divide Road
Larkspur, CO 80118
Office@stonegateresources.org
(www.stonegateresources.com)
(303) 688-5680

Jackson Consulting
Rob Jackson M.S., L.P.C., N.C.C.
500 Lake Street, Suite 105
Excelsior, MN 55331
appointments@ChristianCounsel.com
(www.christiancounsel.com)
(612) 207-7198

Christian Hospital Programs
New Life
1 (800) NEW-LIFE
(www.newlife.com)
Rapha
1 (800) 383-HOPE
(www.rapha-hope.com)

Secular Hospital Programs
The Meadows
1655 N. Tegner St.
Wickenburg, AZ 85390
info@themeadows.org
(www.themeadows.org)
1-800-MEADOWS
Fax: (520) 684-3261

Illinois Institute for Addiction
Recovery at Proctor Hospital
(includes new clinic for comput-
er/Internet addiction)
5409 North Knoxville
Peoria, IL 61614
info@proctor.org
(www.proctor.org/addict.html)
(309) 691-1000

Books

On Spouse's Role in Recovery and Codependency

- *Love Must Be Tough: Straight Talk* by Dr. James C. Dobson (Nashville, Tenn.: Word, 1999)
- *Back from Betrayal: Recovering from His Affairs* by Jennifer P. Schneider, M.D. (New York: Ballantine, 1988)
- *Boundaries* by Henry Cloud and John Townsend (Grand Rapids, Mich.: Zondervan Publishing House, 1992)
- *Safe People* by Henry Cloud and John Townsend (Grand Rapids, Mich.: Zondervan Publishing House, 1996)
- *Codependent No More* by Melody Beattie (New York: HarperCollins Publishers, 1990)

On Computer Addiction

- *Caught in the Net* by Dr. Kimberly Young (New York: John Wiley & Son, 1998)
- *Virtual Addiction: Help For Netheads, Cyberfreaks and Those Who Love Them* by Dr. David Greenfield (Oakland, Calif.: New Harbinger Publications, 1999)

On Gambling Addiction

- *Gambling Addiction: The Problem, the Pain, and the Pathway to Recovery* by John M. Eades (1999) self-published.

- *The Luck Business: The Devastating Consequences and Broken Promises of America's Gambling Explosion* by Robert Goodman (New York: Free Press, 1996)
- *Pathological Gambling: The Making of a Medical Problem* by Brian Castellani (Albany, N.Y.: State University of New York Press, 2000)

On Sex Addiction

- *Living With Your Husband's Secret Wars* by Marsha Means (Grand Rapids, Mich.: Fleming H. Revell, 1999)
- *Love is a Choice* by Robert Hemfelt, Frank Minirth, and Paul Meier (Nashville, Tenn.: Thomas Nelson Publishing, 1989)
- *Women, Sex and Addiction* by Charlotte Davis Kasl (New York: HarperCollins, 1990)
- *Cybersex Exposed: Recognizing the Obsession* by Jennifer P. Schneider and Robert L. Weiss (Minneapolis: Hazelden Publishing and Education, 2001)

Chapter Thirteen

The Payoff

As you finish this book, there may be a little voice in your head asking nagging questions: "Why stop a habit that seems to meet a need, that brings some comfort in an uncomfortable world? Why not just enjoy the habit and try to avoid any negative consequences, just do damage control? Why go through the trouble of recovery—the confession, the withdrawal pains, the struggle?"

The answer depends on what kind of payoff you want to experience in life. Your on-line habit offers you one kind of payoff—an escape, an emotional high, a sense of control, or a numbing effect. Yet, what's the price for that payoff?

A drug called "soma" promised a payoff for the population in Aldous Huxley's book *Brave New World*. The government actually designed the drug and encouraged everyone to use it frequently. "The Brave New Worlders could take holidays from their black moods, or from the familiar annoyances of everyday life," Huxley explains.[1] As you read the book, however, you discover that the government created soma only as a tool to keep the citizens pleasantly numb and euphoric, so they wouldn't seek out God or crave true freedom. Our spiritual enemy promises us little payoffs, small tastes of pleasure, but only so that he can inoculate us from the life God created us to experience.

"The thief comes only to steal and kill and destroy," Jesus tells us. "I have come that they may have life, and have it to the full" (Jn 10:10). Not only does God offer us a full life in the place of the enemy's empty offer, but he also builds us up through the process of struggling against the enemy. Look at Romans 5: "We also rejoice in our sufferings, because we know that suffering produces perseverance; perseverance, character; and character, hope" (Rom 5:3-4). That's the payoff God offers: the richness of life in him and a reward for working to overcome.

So what payoffs can you expect from struggling to overcome your problem? I think there are three key areas of benefit you can expect. The first comes from trading small pleasures for the great joys that God has in store for you. Second, you may see major life changes if you no longer use an addiction to escape from underlying problems but instead tackle those problems head-on. Finally, bringing your Internet use back into balance frees up time and energy, not only for a more productive life but also for you to reach out and help others who share your struggle.

Real Joy

"We are far too easily pleased," says C.S. Lewis in his book *The Weight of Glory:* "We are half-hearted creatures, fooling about with drink and sex and ambition when infinite joy is offered us, like an ignorant child who wants to go on making mud pies in a slum because he cannot imagine what is meant by the offer of a [vacation] at the sea."[2]

The great tragedy of any addiction is that it doles out small pleasures in a way that makes great pleasures more difficult to attain. What great opportunities have you traded for small pleasures—for the rush of an eBay bargain, a virtual jackpot, a winning stock trade, or a conquest in a make-believe game?

Tackling Avoided Problems

The escape, the high, the sense of control, the numbing effect—whatever it is that you've found yourself chasing—is robbing you of a great experience. But it's not just robbing you of real joy; it's robbing you of the joy that can follow pain. The best experiences in life involve overcoming challenges, resolving conflict, exerting effort, and making sacrifices. Addictions pull you away from pain and sacrifice—they encourage you to take the path of least resistance.

I thought about this principle while watching the movie *Remember the Titans*. The movie tells the story of two Virginia high schools that consolidated in the early 1970s and faced the challenges of racial integration. Under the pressure of a demanding coach and a grueling season, the team of black and white players work through ingrained prejudice and emerge as an example of unity for their school and the community.

I heard that an alumnus of the high school complained about the movie's accuracy—something to the effect of, "We were too stoned to pay attention to football back then." If that's true, what did the football players who were forced to work through their differences learn that those who were escaping into a drug-induced high did not?

The addictive high promises to make problems go away, but they're only gone for a moment and then they return, along with guilt, shame, and a feeling of entrapment. Is there a problem you have been trying to escape? The payoff is in overcoming the problem, not in bypassing it.

Helping Others

Recovery from Internet abuse allows you to look past yourself. "Our society is dominated by self-gratification," says Dr. Harry Schaumburg. He believes that recovery requires a shift in focus. The recovering addict needs to ask, "What can I do to serve, to give, to do God's purpose rather than mine?"[3] In David's prayer of repentance, he offers his service to God in exchange for restoration: "Then I will teach transgressors your ways, and sinners will turn back to you" (Ps 51:13).

The last step of traditional twelve-step programs encourages those in recovery to reach out to others who need help. The church needs more people who are recovering from addictions to help those who have just recognized their need.

"Pastors often don't understand this struggle," says Craig Methany, a recovering sex addict. "They need help from those who do."

When Craig hit bottom and got arrested, he told his wife, "I don't know how, but someday God will use this for his glory." Now God is using Craig to call men in his church to purity. Craig warns, however, that people who turn their lives around and then try to help others can fall back into sin if they're not careful. "They need accountability partners and support from their family," he says.[4]

Helping others also means opening old wounds. "You will be more vulnerable," says Brenda, whose husband turned a problem into an outreach. "It will be like tearing off the scab where you have been healing." Yet she feels that moving into a supportive role for others has brought them more healing. "If we wasted our pain, we missed the point," says Brenda. "If I can help one other person address this problem, what I went through would be worth it."[5]

Final Thought

After years of watching the development and hyping of the Internet, writer Clifford Stoll, concluded, "Life in the real world is far more interesting, far more important, far richer, than anything you'll ever find on a computer screen."[6] Remember his words as you work to pull away from the lure of addictive Internet applications.

There is life beyond Internet addiction and there is hope for a restored life beyond the Internet. "I will restore to you the years that the locust hath eaten," God tells his chosen people through the prophet Joel (Jl 2:25, KJV). In God's sovereignty, he can redeem your season of loss and pain.

You can be hopeful that God will lead you not only through recovery but also through transformation. This isn't a time to think about what you are going to lose—the habits you will have to leave behind. It's an opportunity to think about what you can gain—that full and abundant life God promises—starting today.

Notes

INTRODUCTION
Internet Addiction: A Real Problem

1. John M. Grohol, "Internet Addiction Guide", Dr. Grohol's Mental Health Page, last revision December 1999, www.psychcentral.com/netaddiction.
2. Steven Levy, "Breathing Is Also Addictive," *Newsweek,* December 30, 1996/January 6, 1997, 52-53.
3. David Greenfield, telephone conversation with author, September 2000. See also Kathyrn Balint, "Tangled in the Net: Addiction Makes Some Computer Users Virtual Prisoners to Their Web Habit," *San Diego Union-Tribune,* March 12, 2000, D1.
4. Kimberly S. Young, *Caught in the Net* (New York: John Wiley and Son, 1998), 9.
5. Young, 27.
6. Amy E. Nevala, "Addiction to Internet a Growing Problem," *Seattle Post-Intelligencer,* May 20, 2000, A1.
7. Telephone interview with Shane Womack, July 2000.
8. Mark Laaser, *Faithful and True: Sexual Integrity in a Fallen World* (Grand Rapids, Mich.: Zondervan, 1996), 22.

ONE
Trade-Offs: What Addiction Can Do

1. In-person interview with Steve Earll, August 31, 2000.
2. Clifford Stoll, *Silicon Snake Oil: Second Thoughts on the Information Highway* (New York: Anchor, 1995), 13.
3. Stacy Lawrence, "Digital Playground," *Grok,* September 2000, 151. Cyber Dialogue survey results appeared in *Grok* magazine.
4. Michelle Conlin, "Workers Surf at Your Own Risk," *Business Week,* June 12, 2000, 105.
5. Charlotte Faltermayer, "Cyberveillance," *Time,* August 14, 2000, B22.
6. Faltermayer, B22.
7. NFO Worldwide, American Management Association, Vault.com as cited in Conlin, 106.
8. Conlin, 105.
9. Jennifer P. Schneider, "A Qualitative Study of Cybersex Participants: Gender Differences, Recovery Issues, and Implications for Therapists," available online at: www.jenniferschneider.com/articles/qualitative_cybersex.html. Also published in *Sexual Addiction and Compulsivity* 7 (2000): 249-78.
10. In-person interview with Dr. Harry Schaumburg, August 14, 2000.
11. Ellen Gamerman, "Placing Bets Online Easy and Seductive," *Baltimore Sun,* September 22, 1999, Telegraph section, 1A.

12. Email interview with "Chris," June 14, 2000.

13. Prepared testimony of Joseph (Jody) W. Burgin Jr. before the House Committee on Commerce Subcommittee on Telecommunications, Trade and Consumer Protection. Federal News Service, May 23, 2000.

14. Computer Addiction Services, www.computeraddiction.com, Maressa Hecht Orzack, Ph.D.

15. Benedict Carey, "Technology offers better chances for risky liaisons, but it also allows a good shot at prevention," *Los Angeles Times,* July 31, 2000, S-1.

16. Email posting from Julie on Cyber Widows newsgroup. Used by permission.

17. Schneider, "A Qualitative Study of Cybersex Participants."

18. Schneider, "A Qualitative Study of Cybersex Participants."

19. In-person interview with Dr. Steve Fetrow, July 28, 2000.

20. Rebecca Gardyn, "You Can't Download a Hug," *American Demographics,* April 2000; Stanford Institute for the Quantitative Study of Society www.stanford.edu/group/siqss/Press_Release/internetStudy.html.

21. Jennifer P. Schneider, "Effects of Cybersex Addiction on the Family: Results of a Survey", edited by Al Cooper, *Cybersex: The Dark Side of the Force: A Special Issue of the Journal of Sexual Addiction and Compulsivity,* 2000, 43.

22. Interview with Dr. Steve Fetrow.

TWO
The General Lure

---

1. Phone conversation with "Kevin," November 2000.

2. Lawrence, 151.

3. Amy Harmon, "Fighting the Blues? Then Log Off," *Richmond Times,* August 31, 1998, A2; see also homenet.hcii.cs.cmu.edu/progress/research.html.

4. Chuck Colson, "Nothing Like the Real Thing," *Breakpoint,* October 18, 1999.

5. Young, *Caught in the Net,* 20.

6. Young, *Caught in the Net,* 112.

7. Young, *Caught in the Net,* 22.

THREE
The Internet and Money Compulsions

---

1. Kimberly S. Young, "Is Internet Addiction a Problem for You?", AddictionSolutions.com Web site: www.addictionsolutions.com/article_archive/internet_addiction_self.04242000 .00.asp

2. Susan Gregory Thomas, "Getting to Know You.com: How Web Marketers Find

out Shopper's Tastes and Fears to Make the Perfect Sales Pitch," US News Online, November 15, 1999.
www.usnews.com/usnews/issue/991115/nycu/personal.htm.

3. Stoll, 19.
4. Dr. Kimberly Young, email to author, September 12, 2000.
5. Teri Goldberg, "Bidding Till You're Broke," ZDNet News, February 3, 1999.
www.zdnet.com/zdnn/stories/news/0,4586,2200289,00.html.
6. "Online Auction Gains Ground in Local Enterprise Development," *Business World*, May 8, 2000, 26.
7. Erik Hedegaard, "This is Your Brain on eBay," Worth Online, September 1999, www.worth.com/articles/Z9909f03.html.
8. E.S. Browning, "Stock slide apt to bring investing culture 'back to normal,'" *The Wall Street Journal*, October 15, 2000, as cited in *The Denver Post*.
9. Kimberly S. Young, "When Day Trading Becomes a Problem," AddictionSolutions.com Web site:
www.addictionsolutions.com/article_archive/when_day_trading_becomes_problem_05122000.00.asp.
10. Humberto Cruz, "Day Trading Has Nothing to Do With Investing," Tribune Media Services columnist, June 6, 1999, Sacbee Inside Business Finance Web site: www.sacbee.com/ib/finance/cruz/990606.cruz.html.
11. Kimberly S. Young, "Dealing With Compulsive Day Trading—How to Tell When It's Too Much," Center for On-line Addiction Web site: www.netaddiction.com/daytrading.htm.
12. Jeremy Olson, "E-Trading Addiction to Be Focus Signs of Addiction," *Omaha World-Herald*, August 1, 2000, 1.
13. Cruz.
14. Marcy Gordon, "Most People Lose Money in Day Trading, New Report Shows," *Associated Press Business News*, August 9, 2000, Washington dateline.
15. Olson, 1.
16. In-person interview with Marcus Tovar, September 2000.
17. Mark Clothier, "Day Traders Say Shootings 'Not Surprising,'" *Cox News Service*, July 30, 1999, dateline Atlanta.
18. Prepared statement of Chairman Arthur Levitt, United States Securities and Exchange Commission. Subject—Day Trading. Before the Senate Committee on Governmental Affairs Permanent Subcommittee on Investigations, Federal News Service, September 16, 1999.
19. Young, "Dealing With Compulsive Day Trading—How to Tell When It's Too Much."
20. "Prepared testimony of 'John Doe' Internet gambling addict, San Diego, CA" before the House Committee on the Judiciary Subcommittee on Crime Subject—HR 3125, Internet Gambling Prohibition Act of 1999, March 9, 2000.
21. Eugene Martin Christiansen, *An Overview of Gambling in the United States* (New

York: Christiansen/Cummings Associates, Inc., 1998).

22. "The National Gambling Impact Study Commission Final Report," June 1999, "Internet Gambling," Chapter 5, 1.

23. Jim Barlow, "One Profit Center on Net Is Gambling," *Houston Chronicle*, September 19, 2000, Business, 1.

24. *Grok*, 152.

25. Beth Berselli, "Gamblers play the odds online; despite calls to outlaw it, Internet gambling takes off," *The Washington Post*, August 19, 1997, A1.

26. Telephone interview with Dr. Valerie Lorenz, August 2000.

27. Jeff Houck, "Logging in to a Cyber Abyss," *Palm Beach Post*, January 26, 1999, sports section, 1C.

28. Ellen Gamerman, "Placing Bets online easy and seductive," *Baltimore Sun*, September 22, 1999, Telegraph section, 1A.

29. Gamerman, 1A.

30. Telephone interview with Arnie Wexler, August 2000.

FOUR
Games

1. Scott Cohen, *Zap: The Rise and Fall of Atari* (New York: McGraw-Hill, 1984), 29.

2. "Internet Entertainment Users Demand V.I.P. Treatment: Cyber Dialogue Identifies Opportunity for Vertically Integrated Portals," New York, March 1, 1999. www.cyberdialogue.com/news/releases/1999/03-01-cce-portals.html.

3. Bethany Park, "Video Game Addiction on the Rise, Experts Say," *Daily Universe*, via University wire, September 21, 2000, Brigham Young University Dateline, Provo, Utah.

4. Advertisement for Sandbox.com, *Industry Standard*, May 22, 2000, 47.

5. Park.

6. Park.

7. Park.

8. Center for Online Addiction, "Men, Women, and the Internet: Gender Differences," www.netaddiction.com/gender.htm.

9. "Internet Entertainment Users Demand V.I.P. Treatment."

10. Jennifer M. O'Brien, "The games women like to play; industry trend or event," *Computer Dealer News*, March 10, 2000, vol. 16, no. 5, 43.

11. Doctor K, "Healthy Hobby or Addiction?", 1999, www.womengamers.com/articles/inetaddict.html.

12. Balint, D1.

13. Harley Hahn, "Harley Hahn's Guide to Muds," chapter 2, www.harley.com/muds/02.html.

14. Brian Crecente, "In This World of Dungeons and Dragons, Players Make Real Money Roaming a Phony Landscape," *Palm Beach Post*, March 15, 2000, 1D.

15. October 29, 2000, http://cgi.ebay.com/aw-cgi/eBayISAPI.dll?ViewItem&item=477329203, an eBay posting that was available as of Oct. 29, 2000.

16. Crecente, 1D.

17. Ric Manning, "Powerful Force Pulls Addict From Caves of EverQuest," *Louisville* (Ky.) *Courier-Journal,* May 6, 2000, Scene, 2.

18. Jon Tevlin, "In Computer Games, Many Find Release—And an Addiction," *Star Tribune,* December 14, 1999, News, 1A.

19. Tevlin, 1A.

20. Nevala, A1.

21. www.virtual-addiction.com/netstories.htm, available March 2, 2001, The Center for Internet Studies (Dr. Greenfield Web site).

22. Balint, D-1.

23. Doctor K.

FIVE
Relationships

1. Patrick Carnes, *Out of the Shadows: Understanding Sexual Addiction* (Center City, Minn.: Hazelden Information Education, 1992), xiii.

2. Kimberly S. Young, Eric Griffin Shelley, Al Cooper, James O'Mara, and Jennifer Buchanan, "Online Infidelity: A New Dimension in Couple Relationships with Implications for Evaluation and Treatment," *Cybersex: The Dark Side of the Force: A Special Issue of the Journal Sexual Addiction and Compulsivity,* ed. by Al Cooper, 2000, chap. 3, 62-63.

3. Telephone interview with Marnie Ferree, August 2000.

4. Young, et al., 62.

5. Young, et al., 63.

6. Schneider, "A Qualitative Study...."

7. Kimberly S. Young, *Cyber Health Newsletter,* vol. 1, no. 3, delivered via email July 8, 1999.

8. Interview with Dr. Harry Schaumburg.

9. Schneider.

10. Telephone interview with Marnie Ferree, August 2000.

11. Karen S. Peterson, "Spouses Browse Infidelity Online," *USA Today,* July 6, 1999. Available on-line: www.usatoday.com/life/lds002.htm.

12. Peterson.

13. Email posting on Cyber Widows newsgroup. Used by permission.

14. Schneider, "A Qualitative Study...."

15. James C. Dobson, *Love for a Lifetime* (Sisters, Ore.: Multnomah, 1996), 88.

16. Schneider, "A Qualitative Study...."

17. Steve Watters, "Strange Love," July 22, 1999, www.boundless.org/1999/features/90000146.html.

SIX
Porn

1. From email interview with author that first appeared in Steve Watters, "In Your Face, in Your Mind" booklet by Focus on the Family, October, 2000, Dare 2 Dig Deeper Series.
2. Greg Gutfeld, "The Sex Drive," *Men's Health*, October 1999, 118.
3. Jane Kwiatkowski, "Sex addicts pay a heavy price for their compulsions," *The Buffalo News*, August 17, 1999, C1.
4. A. Cooper, D.E. Putnam, L.A. Planchon, and S.C. Boies, "Online Sexual Compulsivity: Getting Tangled in the Net," *Sexual Addiction & Compulsivity* 6, no. 2 (1999): 79-104.
5. Jim Dyar, "Cyber-porn held responsible for increase in sex addiction," *Washington Times*, January 26, 2000. On-line at www.washtimes.com/culture/culture-012600.htm.
6. "Zogby Survey Reveals a Growing Percentage of Those Seeking Sexual Fulfillment on the Internet," Pure Intimacy Web site, March 2000. www.pureintimacy.org/news/a0000031.html.
7. In-person interview with Eldon Fry, August 2000.
8. Howard Unger, "Former Pastor Receives Sentence," *Sarasota Herald-Tribune*, September 12, 2000, A1.
9. Elizabeth Fernandez, "Priest Pleads Guilty to Online Crime," *San Francisco Examiner*, August 27, 2000, Metro, C2.
10. Schneider, "A Qualitative Study of Cybersex Participants."
11. Interview with Marnie Ferree.
12. J. Budziszewski, "Virtual Unfaithfulness: Pornography Use in a Marriage," available at www.pureintimacy.org/online1/essays/a0000032.html.
13. Dyar.
14. Cooper et al., 87.
15. Telephone interview with Dr. Schneider, September 2000.
16. Interview with Eldon Fry.
17. Gutfeld, 119.
18. Schneider.
19. Dyar.
20. In-person interview with Gene McConnell, September 2000.
21. Dyar.
22. Cooper et al., 87.
23. Gary R. Brooks, *The Centerfold Syndrome: How Men Can Overcome Objectification and Achieve Intimacy with Women* (San Francisco: Jossey-Bass, 1995), 12.
24. Brooks, 12.
25. C.S. Lewis, *Mere Christianity* (New York: Macmillan, 1960), 95-96.
26. Testimony of Joseph (Jody) W. Burgin Jr.

27. Interview with Dr. Harry Schaumburg.
28. Email interview, first appeared in Steve Watters, "XXX Files," *New Man* magazine, 2000.
29. Ralph Nader, *Unsafe at Any Speed: The Designed-in Dangers of the American Automobile* (New York: Grossman, 1965).

SEVEN
Overcoming an Internet Addiction

1. Interview with Dr. Harry Schaumburg.
2. Interview with Dr. Steve Fetrow.

EIGHT
A Community of Support

1. Interview with Dr. Steve Fetrow.
2. Young, et al., 71.
3. J.B. email to author, August 21, 2000.
4. Telephone interview with Jennifer Schneider, September 2000.
5. Telephone interview with Rob Jackson, November 20, 2000.
6. Interview with Rob Jackson.
7. Interview with Rob Jackson.
8. In-person interview with Willy Wooten, November 2000.
9. Interview with Dr. Harry Schaumburg.
10. Susan Cheever, "The Healer: Bill Wilson," *Time* Web site, Time 100, Feature. http://www.time.com/time/time100/heroes/profile/wilson01.html.
11. Interview with Rob Jackson.
12. "The Twelve Steps of Alcoholics Anonymous" from the Alcoholics Anonymous World Services, Inc. Web site. On-line at www.alcoholics-anonymous.org/english/E_FactFile/M-24_d6.html.
13. "Is it proper for Christians to attend Alcoholics Anonymous meetings and use the 12 steps and AA literature?" Christian Recovery Connection Frequently Asked Questions, http://crc.iugm.org/faq.html.
14. Interview with Willy Wooten.
15. "How do support groups help the struggling addict?" Christian Recovery Connection Frequently Asked Questions, http://crc.iugm.org/faq.html.
16. Interview with Willy Wooten.
17. Interview with Marnie Ferree.
18. Schneider, "A Qualitative Study of Cybersex Participants."
19. Interview with Marnie Ferree.

20. Interview with Rob Jackson.
21. Telephone interview with Zach Britton, October 2000.
22. Interview with Dr. Schaumburg.
23. Interview with Rob Jackson.

NINE
Addressing Behavior

1. Stephen R. Covey, *The Seven Habits of Highly Effective People* (New York: Simon and Schuster, 1989), 136-38.

TEN
Addressing Head and Heart

1. C. Cummings, J.R. C. Gordon, and G.A. Marlatt, (1980). "Relapse: Prevention and Prediction," in W.R. Miller, ed., *The Addictive Behaviors: Treatment of Alcoholism, Drug Abuse, Smoking and Obesity* (New York: Pergamon, 1980), 291-321.
2. Cooper et al, 87.
3. Nevala, A1.
4. Interview with Dr. Schaumburg.
5. Interview with Dr. Steve Fetrow.
6. Interview with Dr. Schaumburg.
7. In-person interview with Steve Earll, August 31, 2000.
8. Claudia Black, *Double Duty* (New York: Ballantine, 1990), 12.
9. Interview with Steve Earll.

ELEVEN
Restoring Relationship With God

1. Telephone interview with Rob Jackson, October 2000.
2. Telephone interview with Rob Jackson, March 6, 2001.
3. Interview with Dr. Steve Fetrow.
4. John Eldredge, *The Journey of Desire* (Nashville, Tenn.: Thomas Nelson, 2000), 84.
5. Brent Curtis and John Eldredge, *The Sacred Romance*, (Nashville, Tenn.: Thomas Nelson, 1997), 133.
6. Email interview with Craig Methany, October 11, 2000.
7. Interview with Dr. Steve Fetrow.
8. Interview with Steve Earll.
9. Interview with Rob Jackson.

TWELVE
Practical Steps for the Person Concerned

1. James C. Dobson, *Love Must Be Tough: Straight Talk* (Nashville, Tenn.: Word, 1999), 30.
2. Kimberly S. Young, "Is Internet addiction a problem for someone you know?," Addiction Solutions web site at www.addictionsolutions.com/article_archive/internet_addiction_other.042420 00.00.ASP.
3. Interview with Dr. Jennifer Schneider.
4. Interview with Rob Jackson.
5. Interview with Rob Jackson.
6. Interview with Dr. Jennifer Schneider.
7. Interview with Marnie Ferree.
8. Interview with Dr. Steve Fetrow.
9. Interview with Steve Earll.
10. Telephone interview with Marsha Means, September 2000.
11. Telephone interview, September 2000.
12. Interview with Marsha Means.
13. Dobson, 30.
14. Interview with "Brenda."
15. Interview with Marsha Means.
16. Interview with Dr. Harry Schaumburg.
17. Telephone interview with Dr. Valerie Lorenz, August 2000.

THIRTEEN
The Payoff

1. Aldous Huxley, *Brave New World Revisited* (New York: Harper and Row, 1958), 82.
2. C.S. Lewis, *The Weight of Glory and Other Addresses,* revised and expanded edition, (New York: MacMillan, 1949), 3-4.
3. Interview with Dr. Harry Schaumburg.
4. Email interview with Craig Methany, September 11, 2000.
5. Interview with "Brenda."
6. Stoll, 13.